An Extremely Dangerous Piece of Lint

Jeri Kroll

Blue Boat Books

IPSWICH, MASSACHUSETTS

Lisa – Thanks for being you! I look forward to reading your book!

JERI

Blue Boat Books
46 Argilla Rd.
Ipswich, Massachusetts/USA 01983
krolljeri@gmail.com

Publisher's Note: This is a work of fiction. Names, characters, places, and incidents are a product of the author's imagination. Locales and public names are sometimes used for atmospheric purposes. Any resemblance to actual people, living or dead, or to businesses, companies, events, institutions, or locales is completely coincidental.

Book Layout © 2017 BookDesignTemplates.com

Cover Design by Patch Kroll

An Extremely Dangerous Piece of Lint/Jeri Kroll. -- 1st ed.
ISBN 978-1-7320804-0-9

Dedicated to

My partner – Jodi
My family – Barry, Kathy, Patch and David
Longtime friends – Rosa, Midge and Deb, Donna
and Anne
Furry friends past and present –Jacob, Benjamin,
Simon and Suzie
Super therapist – Jan
All the folks at the Northshore Unitarian
Universalist Church, Danvers, MA

"You can't go back and change the beginning, but you can start where you are and change the ending."

C.S. Lewis

Preface

The short essays and poems in this collection were written over the course of nearly four decades. As I set about the task of compiling them, I realized how my voice has changed over the years. I did not include some of my early depressing pieces but there is a hint of those dark days in a few of them! As the years have progressed my writing has become filled with more humor and it is obvious I have moved to place where, thankfully, I don't take myself so seriously.

Age has also brought on a penchant for swearing – I'm not sure why but if you, the reader, are offended by those words or phrases then by all means please substitute your favorite non-swear – gosh all fish hooks, son of a biscuit ... whatever works for you!

These pieces are purposefully not arranged chronologically in the order in which they were written. In reviewing the manuscript, I realize this may leave a reader feeling a bit discombobulated. I prefer, however, to bounce around from one iteration of myself to another without constraint. On a positive note, you may choose to start at the end of the book and work backwards. Or you could start somewhere in the middle. Since no-one gets murdered, it really doesn't matter.

Many of the short essays contain thoughts related to being a Unitarian Universalist which has been a major factor in shaping who I am or maybe I should say who I want to be. Unitarian Universalists accept all the religions as pathways to a spiritual journey. We have no single creed one must accept in order to belong.

We try to live in the world guided by these principles:

1. The inherent worth and dignity of every person.
2. Justice, equity and compassion in human relations.
3. Acceptance of one another and encouragement to spiritual growth.
4. A free and responsible search for truth and meaning.
5. The right of conscience and the use of the democratic process within our congregations and in society at large.
6. The goal of world community with peace, liberty and justice for all.
7. Respect for the interdependent web of all existence of which we are a part.

I hope these pieces provide encouragement for you to examine your own existence and in so doing experience that humor is a magnificent healer.

Contents

Jeri Kroll

1: An Extremely Dangerous Piece of Lint

Most people I know have a fear of something even if it doesn't reach the level of a diagnosable phobia. My fear comes close – close enough that I've tried to analyze its roots in therapy but to no avail. I remain, and I assume I will always remain absolutely petrified of wasps – not bees, not hornets, not flying insects in general – wasps. Don't get me wrong, I'll avoid a honey bee but if they're minding their own sweet, cute little business of gathering nectar and pollinating the flowers, I'm good with that. Wasps? There is nothing, I repeat, nothing cute or sweet or good about a wasp. The sight of one anywhere - on the side of a building on a warm spring day, high up in the eaves flying in and out of their ugly nests, batting against a window pane inside the house where they don't belong, can only mean one thing – run, flail, scream.

The worst of all situations is when a wasp is in the car. Once when I was a passenger in the front seat a wasp dropped in my lap when I pulled down the sun visor. I literally had one foot out the door of the vehicle traveling 60 miles an hour down a highway when the driver (thank the Lord Jesus) grabbed me with one hand and pulled me back into the car.

Many years ago, I was a passenger in the back seat of a car traveling with three other professionals to an important meeting. The hairs on the back of my head stood up as I heard that low buzzing sound of a wasp. When I looked around to see one fluttering around against the back window I hollered, "Stop the car NOW!" at which time I simultaneously hurled myself over the front seat across the lap of the front seat passenger and onto the floor. I crouched down on all fours covering my head while continuing to scream, "Stop the car, stop the car." I have no idea why my career continued to progress.

The interesting phenomenon is that once I've spotted a wasp anything that looks or sounds remotely like a wasp totally freaks me out. Because of this I have frequently been the butt of well-deserved teasing. When I jump, run, scream or swat at something which is harmless I try to act as nonchalant as I can – like when you get up after a fall and act as if nothing happened. Once when I was sitting on our front porch with a few friends, a perceived wasp-like foreign object flew past me. As I screamed and flailed I noticed that it was a piece of lint. With a familiar smirk on her face my partner asked me, "What was that?" I straightened up and responded confidently as if stating a scientific fact, "It was an extremely dangerous piece of lint." Obviously, they all should have been thankful I took the proper precautions to deal with the dangerous intruder.

2

When I think about the effects of fear I am reminded of FDR's famous line, "The only thing we have to fear is fear itself." He was talking about economics and trying to convince people not to panic and take all their money out of the banks. That concept, however, has a broader application.

It's the end of 2017. Our country, the "United" States, is divided by fear – fear of anything "other" – immigrants, blacks, Muslims, gays. The dangerous fact is that fear quickly translates into hatred. We fear and then we hate. I hate wasps. I really do. They should be exterminated. They have no place on our houses, inside our homes, in our cars. They are ugly, dangerous, useless pieces of shit.

There are people trying to address the hatred in our country. Perhaps we need to face ours fear. How to do that, I assume, would take many different paths. All I have to offer here is just the simple thought that when it comes to humans:

There are no inherently dangerous pieces of lint – only people.

An Extremely Dangerous Piece of Lint

2: Hi, How are You?

Everybody knows that when we greet acquaintances or colleagues by saying, "Hi, how are you?", the "how are you" part is not really a question. When we say, "Hi, how are you?" we're really saying, "Hi, hi."

Why do we use such a redundant way of greeting each other?

Most often the response to the question "how are you" is a rote, "Fine", having nothing whatever to do with how the person thinks he or she is. The grammatically correct among us are fond of saying, "I'm well, thank you."

Occasionally, someone challenges the question by asking, "Do you really want to know?" The reality of our intent probably falls somewhere in the middle. "Well, I wouldn't mind knowing a couple of sentences worth of stuff but certainly not a whole chapter's worth." Sometimes the worst thing happens, and the person answers the question with disturbing details about some nasty physical ailment. At that point you're in real trouble and must get out of the conversation as quickly as possible.

My question is, if a person is really asking how I am, what does that mean? How am I? How is my life situation as I perceive it to be? How am I physically as far as I know? How am I emotionally, as in, how do I feel? Lately, when someone says to me "Hi, how are you," I answer honestly by saying, "I don't know." I don't know if I am about to be laid off from work or if I'm about to find out I have a terminal illness. I don't know how I am. How could I?

Sometimes instead of saying "I don't know," I say, "I'm fine as far as I know." Or "In my opinion, I'm fine." The latter two seem to amuse people while the "I don't know" response somehow seems to alienate them. For example, yesterday, when I saw a colleague at work in our mail room, she greeted me by saying blandly, "Hi, how are you?" I responded flatly, "There's really no way to know." I interpreted her facial expression as something close to a scowl as she whirled around and left the room.

So, if we rule out saying "Hi, how are you?" then what do we say? It seems somehow unnatural not to ask some sort of question. But, the alternatives aren't much better:

Question: Hi, what's up?

Answer: I don't know but eventually it will come down.

Question: Hi, how's it going?

Answer: Depends if I'm pointed in the right direction.

Question: Hi, isn't this a beautiful day?

Answer: I was really hoping for a nor'easter, so I wouldn't have to leave the house.

Here's an idea. Why don't we give up this ridiculous, meaningless how-are-you business and greet each other exclusively with statements like these: "Hi, it's really good to see you this morning" or "Hi, you look great today." The problem here, of course, is if you don't have anything positive to say. I mean you can't say, "Hi, another bad hair day, I see" or "Hi, I see you've gotten another hideous tongue piercing."

One other alternative would be to stop greeting each other verbally altogether and simply wave or possibly, when appropriate, give the two thumbs up sign. These gestures would generate a positive, welcoming feeling without the pressure for one to analyze his or her state of being or to come up with something nice to say about the other person.

I think I'll try it. Next time I meet acquaintances or colleagues I'll greet them with a friendly wave and leave it at that.

An Extremely Dangerous Piece of Lint

3: Five Decades Later

Wouldn't go back a day,

A month, a year.

"Come too far," I say,

"It's absurd that I made it to here!"

Five decades wrought,

I look ahead.

More likely than not,

Five more: I'm dead!

An Extremely Dangerous Piece of Lint

4: Found Money

About twelve years ago I started picking up coins I found while jogging. In those days I had been in the practice of never breaking my stride for anything much less a chewed-up penny. But one day there they were - three shiny dimes all lined up in a row ahead of me. I know precisely where they were located – on what street, on which side of the road, by what house. "Why am I passing by 30 cents?" I thought. I picked up the coins and to my delight also found a nickel and three pennies later all of which I carefully placed in my shorts pocket.

That was the beginning. Since that day I have placed all "found money" in a special jar to be counted at the end of the year. After December 31st I record the yearly total as well as how many of each coin or the occasional bill I have collected.

The process of successfully finding and retrieving a coin requires a variety of skills. First, obviously, you spot something in the road or on the sidewalk and suspect it might be a coin. As you get closer you continue to assess its shape, color, thickness, shininess. There are a lot of things that look like coins from a distance. The two most despicable of these are spittle and bird poop. Where I live seagull poop is especially prevalent. How the gull manages to land its excrement in such perfectly shaped little circles is one of life's great mysteries. Obviously, it is extremely important to develop your observational skills so that you only reach down for an actual coin. Early in my career I could be seen reaching down then lurching back violently. If my hand came close to touching some vile substance, an expletive would also erupt from deep within me. I looked like a wanna-be runner with Tourette's syndrome.

For a period of time I began overcompensating by running past a coin for fear that I had not accurately assessed the object's nature. That approach did little to improve my image. After realizing I had in fact run past a coin, I had to come to a screeching halt, run backwards and try to relocate the object. That sounds easy, but it isn't. Often you just can't spot the coin again. You run forwards and backwards numerous times trying to stop in the exact location where you saw the money in the first place, but no luck. Once when this occurred in front of the city's senior center, an elderly gentleman on the bench out front thought I was destitute and asked if I needed money. I gave up the "running-past" tactic fairly quickly. Fortunately, my skills improved, and I became adept at accurately assessing early on what was or was not an actual coin.

The next step in the process is the most exciting - determining what type of coin it is. Is it a penny or a dime? It's about the size of a penny but it seems a little shinier. Is it a nickel or a quarter?

Over the years what you notice about found money is the disproportionate number of pennies you find.

It's near the end of August and here's my YTD status:

112 pennies

19 nickels

0 dimes

15 quarters

0 bills

and 1 Turkish kuru (which

unfortunately, doesn't count)

That's a total of 177 coins equaling $8.82.

Here comes the serious part. What occurs to me is that often times we treat people the same way we treat found money. Most of the pennies I find have obviously spent a long time being run over, stepped on, kicked under piles of debris – chewed up, disfigured, disregarded – barely recognizable as a coin. Quarters, on the other hand, are most often in excellent shape. Even a non-found money collector will stop to pick up a quarter whereas he or she would never condescend to stoop for a measly penny.

Where I work we have people who are pennies and we have people who are quarters. Some of the quarters like to constantly point out that they are quarters and should be treated as such. The pennies get together in small groups to express their disdain for the quarters who oppress them. Of course, there are also dimes and nickels. I'm like a dime at work. I have quarters above me who make decisions about whether I'll be laid off and make the determination about how valuable I am to the company. Getting rid of a dime or two can save the company some money. There are also nickels and pennies below me. Some of the pennies definitely look chewed up and spit out.

An Extremely Dangerous Piece of Lint

I was in the mail room the other day when a quarter and a penny came in to the room at the same time. My survival instincts told me to acknowledge and interact with the quarter and ignore the penny. As a person who, for good or ill, constantly assesses what I am thinking, feeling and doing, I almost immediately felt ashamed of my reaction. "You're a Unitarian Universalist, for God's sake," I thought. "The penny and the quarter should both be treated with respect and dignity."

A lot of people think Unitarian Universalism is easy because we can believe whatever we want and none of us are going to hell and we don't have to go to church in the summer. That's not true. Well, the parts about not going to hell and not going to church in the summer are true, but I would contend that being a Unitarian Universalist is not easy. We may not have a creed we need to buy in to, but we do have principles. One of them is the belief in the inherent worth and dignity of every person. Maybe, as with all religions, it isn't the professing of a belief or a principle that's the hard part but the practicing of it.

What if I tried an experiment, I thought, and for just one day I treated every person with whom I interacted as if I absolutely believed he or she had value? Part of the goal would be for the people to experience the fact that they were being treated a bit differently, so that after the interaction they would scratch their heads and say, "Gee, she treated me as if I was a quarter!"

14

After writing this piece, I decided to scrounge through my found money collection and take out the most damaged, beat up penny I could find. I brought that penny to work with me as a reminder of my values and efforts to live by my UU principles. After two days one of my colleagues looked quizzically at me and asked, "What happened to you? You're all positive all of a sudden." "Gosh," I thought. "I guess I've been more negative in my attitude toward people than I realized!" At least I was apparently meeting with some success at reforming myself.

So, next time you come across a penny – a real penny that is – I would ask you not to stop and pick it up. Trust me you don't want to start lurching and swearing and running backward. The found money thing is addictive and nobody wants to fight another addiction. But, next time you see a penny, especially a worn-out, chewed-up, beat-up one, whatever your religious background or absence of one, ask yourself, "How am I treating people these days?"

An Extremely Dangerous Piece of Lint

5: The Bassetts

November 13, 2017

Today is the first day of my retirement. I've heard stories from those who have preceded me. Some returned to work shortly after retiring because they no longer felt vital. Others seem to have made a healthy adjustment to life without the daily grind. While I'm fairly certain I won't fall into the first camp of returners, I do worry a bit that all I'll have to talk about at the end of the day is whether or not the two basset hounds were outside in their fenced yard when I walked our dog past them. This encounter precipitates a great deal of excitement on the part of the canines – lots of barking, growling, snorting, sniffing, all while jumping up and down. Even before retirement when I'd get home first to walk the dog my report would include, "the bassets were out" or "the bassets weren't out today." Of course, there is other dog-talk regarding things like the number of times pooping occurred and the consistency thereof, but the bassets are always the most interesting news.

This morning when I was out walking the thought occurred to me that if someone didn't know differently he or she might assume the bassets were our elderly neighbors. A quick Google search revealed that the last name "Bassett" is in fact prevalent in Massachusetts where I live. In 1635 one William Bassett was an early immigrant to New England.

Through the years there have been famous Bassetts in virtually every field – academia, politics, the arts, sports, religion, the military, and so on.

I think I'd name our imaginary human Bassetts George and Mary. I would embellish the account of my dog walk by saying, "The Bassetts were out this morning. Mary says she and George are hosting Thanksgiving this year and the kids are all coming." I would be prepared with the names of each of the children and where they live – maybe throw in a grandchild or two. I think I'd stick to no more than three children living in two different states and no more than two grandkids. Keeping these details straight would be important to the integrity of my story.

Of course, if I grew weary of George and Mary since really, let's face it, they are pretty boring, the Bassetts could be the gay couple down the street who recently adopted a little girl from China. Or they could be the African American family in town who put a "Black Lives Matter" banner in their yard. The Bassetts would open up a whole world of conversation about politics, religion, and social action.

In reality, I wouldn't allow myself to engage in such telling of tales, as entertaining as that might be. I try to be a good Unitarian Universalist. Our fourth principle is *not* the reckless and irresponsible search for truth and meaning. Clearly, I can't rely on the Bassetts whoever they are to give my life meaning. At day's end like a good UU I'll continue my free and responsible search for truth and meaning without the bassets – may they "em-bark" on their own spiritual journey – blessed be!

18

6: Space Issues

Some people take up

A L O T   O F   S P A C E.

i'dliketotakeupsomespace.

not a lot
just a little

Just enough to feel that I have the right

to be seen
and heard
and felt.

Maybe even to be taken into account

I don't need a lot of space

Just a little

At least enough

To know that I'm alive.

From:
21 Inspirational Quotes That Everyone Needs to
Stop Using Immediately
Jenna Mullins in E! News

Five of Them:

"Life is what happens to you while you're busy making
other plans."
*Jokes on you, we don't make plans. We stay indoors
watching Netflix.*

"You have to look through the rain to see the rainbow."
Or you can just look through the window.

"Shoot for the moon. Even if you miss, you'll land among
the stars."
*This is scientifically inaccurate. The closest star is 93 mil-
lion miles away. It's called the sun. Perhaps you've heard
of it.*

It takes more muscles to frown than it does to smile."
*Yeah, but it takes zero muscles to stare blankly at you until
you go away.*

7: I Beg to Differ

By definition, I suppose, it would be a bit bizarre for someone to say he or she likes hackneyed expressions. Synonyms for hackneyed, according to Merriam Webster, are banal, commonplace, stale, moth-eaten, tired, trite. Antonyms are fresh, new, novel, original. Aside from a strong preference to being original over being moth-eaten, hackneyed expressions, aka, clichés, make me feel argumentative. I'd like to think it has something to do with being a Unitarian Universalist and our free and responsible search for truth and meaning. Clichés often-times conceptualize reality in absolutes using or implying the word "always" or "never." "Always" and "never" are generally not popular UU words. For example, the grass isn't always greener on the other side of the fence and the early bird doesn't always get the worm. Sometimes, thankfully, the apple does fall far from the tree and it's not a small world it's actually rather large after all. I'm not sure why you'd want to look a gift horse in the mouth, but I think you should be allowed to. The shoe may fit but I just might choose not to wear it. And besides that, some who wander are lost and maybe the glass is half-empty – just sayin'.

Rhetorical questions have much the same effect on me. I want to argue the opposite of the implied answer. "What were you thinking?" I don't know but at least I was thinking something. Or "how's that working out for you?" Fine, thank you. It's working out just fine.

An Extremely Dangerous Piece of Lint

One common phrase I find interesting to explore is "I beg to differ." When I searched for the origins of "begging to differ," I discovered a consensus that the phrase is considered archaic. The sentiment seems to be "just say you disagree and be done with the faux polite begging bull shit."

I like that! As UUs we don't beg to differ, we revel in it. Our phrase might be "I'm so pleased to differ with you." It sounds quite pleasant actually and I don't think it leaves folks like me feeling oppositional or argumentative. So next time someone talks to me about early birds with worms or big mouthed horses with gifts I just might say, "I am so pleased to differ with you." I'll smile knowing they think I'm a lunatic, but I'll know that I'm just a good UU.

8: Midlife Crisis

Trapped by success,

Married to the avoidance of pain,

Godforsaken midlife mediocrity.

Lack of courage,

Pathetically predictable patterns,

Wasted potential.

Who is that person in the mirror

staring back at me?

Nobody I ever wanted to be.

"'I do love it when I am right,' Hyacinth said triumphantly. 'Which is fortunate, since I so often am.'"

Julia Quinn

9: You're Wrong

Of course, there are times when I am wrong about something. But here's the thing – if I think I'm wrong about something I'll change my mind so then I'm right. Which means that at any given moment, I kind of think I'm right about most everything which of course is wrong!

What I wonder about is at what point does a person realize they may be wrong? Is it when something comes to their attention more than five times? More than three? Only once? That seems a bit hasty!

And where's the balance? It seems unnatural to go around thinking you're wrong about everything just as it's clearly pompous to go around thinking you're right about everything. Maybe just split it 50/50 and call it a day?

Maybe what's wrong is that we even think in terms of right and wrong. Wouldn't it be better when discussing the facts to say something like, "My current understanding is this?" That might be a good approach even in those situations where you know you are absolutely 100% correct. Here's an example.

About fifteen years back, I was training to run a 10-mile road race during Newburyport's Yankee Homecoming Days, when both a 5K and a 10-mile race occur the same evening. I had participated in the

5K many times but had been preparing myself for about a year to run the longer race. The 10-mile course is very tough, with two of the last three miles being one long continuous unshaded stretch through marshland. Races with bends and turns and houses are helpful because you can say to yourself, "Just make it to that house with the picket fence, that's all you need to do," and after that "just make to that bend in the road three blocks down, it's just three blocks, you can do it." Long, houseless stretches definitely demand extra mental toughness.

About two weeks prior to the event, I happened to mention to a co-worker that I was running in the race. She exclaimed, "Oh, I live on High Street in Newburyport, the 10K goes right past my apartment." I foolishly decided to correct her and said, "Actually it's 10 miles, not 10K." She replied, "Oh no, it's a 10K". God help me, I couldn't let it go, partly, of course, because of pride but also because she was a person who thought she was right about everything and had the IQ of an amoeba. "I've been training for the race," I said. "It's 10 miles, not a 10K. 10K is 6.2 miles." "Oh, no" said the amoeba. "I've watched that race from my apartment and it's 10K." Still I persisted. "I'm telling you, I've been training for nearly a year and it's 10 miles." At that point she shot me a hostile glance, took a deep breath and shook her head as if she felt sorry for me in my ignorance. And so it was that all of my Unitarian Universalist values were totally compromised by thoughts of inflicting serious bodily harm. As I stood there contemplating which form of bodily harm would give the most pleasure, I realized this was one of those no-win arguments and that engaging further would cast doubts about my own

26

intelligence. "Step away from the amoeba," I told myself – obviously not quite ready to embrace the concept of the inherent worth and dignity of *every* person.

I realize in hindsight that the whole interaction could have been avoided and I would have felt like a much better UU if I had simply said, "It's my understanding the race is 10 miles." She would probably have just shrugged her shoulders and walked away knowing I was mistaken. I would have walked away knowing she was mistaken. And so the world would return to its usual state of affairs with all of us walking around thinking we're right.

An Extremely Dangerous Piece of Lint

10: A Sign

For several weeks in November while I was out jogging, I had been drawn to a holiday decoration – a 12-inch-high Santa Claus – in the window of the House of the Raven, a great little gift shop on Main Street. in downtown Gloucester, Massachusetts. Each time I jogged past the store the attraction intensified. Since I don't carry any money on me when I run, this ruled out the option of going into the store at the time and purchasing the Santa. And so, we continued for some time, he and I, looking at each other through the window longingly.

The thought occurred to me one evening that a normal person would grab some money, hop in the car and go back to the store. You'd think that would be one of life's easy decisions, but you would be wrong! On the one hand, we always go into the House of the Raven after the holidays to get merchandise half-off, so it would make sense to wait a few weeks and hope that my Santa would still be there. On the other hand, it's good to support your local businesses and maybe I should make a full-price purchase every now and then. On the other hand, I was in a serious downsizing mode and I really didn't need the decoration. On the other hand, it wouldn't be a bad idea to add the Santa to my collection. I have three holiday collections, which are reindeer (or moose), snowmen, and Santas. When I put out these decorations the collections must reside in different areas of the condo. A moose must not comingle with a snowman or God forbid a Santa with a moose. My Santa collection is by far the smallest because, let's be honest, most Santas are hideous.

Ultimately, I decided that I was incapable of making a decision ... on the one hand, on the other hand, on yet another hand. My hands were tired. Clearly what I needed was a sign. I decided to drive down Main Street after work one evening and in the unlikely event a parking place opened up right near the shop, I'd take it as a sign I should take the spot, go in and purchase the Santa. I drove slowly down Main Street that first evening with faith that a parking space would miraculously materialize. But, no, no spot, no sign, no Santa.

A couple of days later I decided to give it another try. I drove so slowly down Main Street, again, having faith that this would allow sufficient time for a spot to pen up, that the vehicle behind me started honking angrily with long, shrill blasts. In the spirit of the holiday I lowered my window, hollered "Fuck you," and flipped him off for good measure. Clearly, he didn't understand anything about signs and faith and had no spiritual depth whatsoever. But once again – no spot, no sign, no Santa.

But I was not to be deterred – I hate clichés but isn't there supposed to be something charming about three? And in fact, there was. No, I did not find a parking space on my third attempt, but now I understood – I was overjoyed by the revelation – this *was* the sign. It was a sign that I should go home, leave the car and walk back to the store to purchase the Santa. And that's exactly what I did!

As I was walking back home with my prized possession safely tucked under my arm, however, it
occurred to me that looking for a sign is so distinctly
non-UU- like, isn't it? We use our brains; we make
intelligent decisions based on facts. We do not look
for signs. We are not swept away by holiday senti-
mentality. We think; we're rational, we're smart!

So maybe the Santa episode was not my finest UU
moment but each year now when I place the Santa
in his designated spot I laugh and reminisce with
him about how we came to cohabitate. I tell him I
really do want to be a better UU and he supports
my resolve in silent acceptance.

11. Just Me

"It's just me" is my usual greeting,
But it isn't a put-down.
"Just me" means,
"It's safe! Relax."

It's just me:
no threat;
no judgment;
no need to flex your muscles.

It's just me:
liberal;
accepting;
a Unitarian Universalist for God's sake!

For any of you who may object to my greeting,
"It's just me,"
As far as I'm concerned,
"Just me" is just fine.

"I know nothing except the fact of my igno-rance."

Socrates

12: Epistemology

Last week while feeling that life was great,

I learned that feeling did not match my fate:

My job was in jeopardy; I lost my dog;

My wife turned out to be dense as a log.

Today while feeling as down as a goose,

I learned that feeling was also a ruse:

I got a promotion; my dog came back;

My wife ran off with my cousin, Jack.

Our feelings come; our feelings go.

Reality's somewhere mixed up in the flow.

We feel as we think; we think as we feel;

The question is how do we know what is real?

"A lot of people don't like bumper stickers. I don't mind bumper stickers. To me a bumper sticker is a shortcut. It's like a little sign that says. 'Hey, let's never hang out.'"

Demetri Martin

13: Bumper Stickers

There ought to be some laws regarding bumper stickers. Yesterday I almost rear ended the car in front of me while trying to read his. That's wrong! If you put a bumper sticker on your vehicle it should at least be big enough to read at a safe distance. Outlawing bumper stickers altogether would make the most sense but I'm not sure that would have enough grassroots support. If not made illegal however, there could at least be some rules and regulations. Here would be my seven:

All bumper stickers must:

1. Adhere to a Standard Font Size
   First and foremost, bumper stickers should not endanger our lives. All bumper stickers should be large enough to read from at least a car length away. Experts in the field of ophthalmology would determine what font size should be the standard.

2. Be Pertinent to Current Events
   A grace period of 90 days would be allowed for the proper removal of all bumper stickers that no longer pertain to current events. For example, I actually saw a W 04 sticker on a car the other day. Of course, putting it on the vehicle in the first place shows poor judgment but by law it should be removed and shredded.

3. Not Be Located on the Bumper
Perhaps it renders the term "bumper sticker" an oxymoron but bumper stickers should not be placed on the bumper. A better location would be on a window in a spot that does not obstruct the driver's vision. Stickers affixed to the body of the car are not easily removed making compliance with the rules around bumper stickers more difficult to follow. Besides that, if you try to sell your car, finding a person who agrees with your political ideology, loves German Shepherds, has a kid who is an honor student and has Jesus as his co-pilot could make it impossible to find the right buyer.

4. Be Limited in Number
Any more than three to five bumper stickers on one vehicle brings into question the bodily integrity of that vehicle. Besides that, how many things about yourself or issues does one person have the right to put out there in everybody's face? Five is generous.

5. Not Be X-rated
Come on, some bumper stickers should not be seen by anyone under the age of ... under the age of 90.

6. Not Declare Your Love
I ♥ My Cat. I ♥ my Boston Terrier. I ♥ my Appaloosa. Come on. Nobody cares. Express your love to them and leave it off the car.

7. Not Indicate Who's in the Vehicle
Sometimes it's a little sign but it's the same principle. Caution: Baby on Board. Caution: Show Dogs on Board. So, I should get in to an accident with a vehicle that doesn't specify who's on board? I'd like to display one that says I'm on Board. Besides that, I'm sure those precious passengers are not always on board every trip. Those vehicles should be pulled over periodically like a commercial truck pulling into a weigh station. If the specified passengers are nowhere to be found, there should definitely be a fine imposed on the driver for making the rest of us unduly cautious.

I could come up with more regulations, but I've already given more time and thought to bumper stickers than they deserve. Without fleshing out all the rules, my simple request would be this: if you are about to place a sign or bumper sticker on your vehicle, stop for a minute and ask yourself, "Why?"

"There may be as much nobility in being last as in being first, because the two positions are equally necessary in the world, the one to compliment the other."

Jose Ortega Y Gasset

14: Somebody's Got to Be Last

I've always been a wannabe runner. My weight and stature have never been my allies in this pursuit, but year after year, I have persisted in running – running alone, running with partners, running in the early morning hours, running in the wind and the rain, running in road races.

I was running in a road race quite a few years ago early in the season. It was a very hilly, tough 10K in Rockport, Massachusetts and I had never run the course before. Usually in any given road race I end up jostling back and forth with a number of "back-of-the-packers" but on this particular occasion I quickly became a pack of one and had lost track of all the other runners in the race. As I rounded a bend in the road and faced a very steep, long hill ahead of me, I spotted the race volunteer at the top of the hill with her flag poised to point me in the right direction. I was both relieved and pressured by her presence. On the one hand, it was good to know I would not get lost on the course – at least not yet. On the other hand, I felt I needed to prove that I was not a complete loser by running up the damn hill as fast as I could. My ascent was, in fact, torturously slow as I glanced up periodically to be sure the volunteer was still there with her arms crossed wearing a "how-long-can-it-possibly-take-a-human-to-get-up-this-hill" expression on her face. When I finally made it to the top, she snapped her flag left and declared in an unsympathetic, matter-of-fact tone, "Somebody's got to be last."

Those words have stayed with me over the years and though clearly her intent was not to cheer me on, the race volunteer had unwittingly provided just the words of encouragement I've needed on many occasions. It was the word "somebody" that caught my attention. I was somebody. I know what it's like to feel like a nobody – deadly! But to be somebody – okay, maybe a last-place somebody but a somebody - I can live with that. Somebody does have to be last! I'm not a loser – I'm filling a valuable role that, let's face it, not everyone can embrace.

This morning I was out running alone – a wonderful five mile run along the backshore of Gloucester, Massachusetts. At this point I "ralk" which is my word for alternating between running and walking but I'm still the same old wannabe runner. As I was critically taking stock of my ralk – how far, how fast, the ratio of running to walking – I initially felt a bit discouraged. But then I remembered the words of the unintentionally supportive race volunteer and with that threw my arms into the air in a sign of victory and proudly shouted aloud, "Somebody's got to be last ... and it's me!"

15: Immortality

(upon completion of a long-distance run)

Dad would've been proud,
A glimmer of light.
Reality uttered out loud,
"Yeah, right."

Too slow, too fast;
Too fat, too thin;
Come first or last,
No way to win.

So now that Dad's been long gone dead,
I'm left to judge myself instead.
Too often harsh, too seldom fair,
Without a doubt my father's heir.

An Extremely Dangerous Piece of Lint

16: Free at Last

Many fast food restaurant chains offer coupon booklets for a donation to some worthy cause. While I'm sure this does benefit the charity, it clearly benefits the restaurant by encouraging costumers to return to their dining establishments with their super bargain coupons – buy one, get one free, $10 off a meal for four, buy a big old greasy cheeseburger and get a free extra-large fry to speed up the process of arterial clogging, and so on.

I'm a sucker for giving to charities. This is why I never answer my phone anymore. One week of answering the telephone could cost me upwards of $100. There are two chain restaurants that I frequent, both of which regularly offer coupon booklets in exchange for a donation to a well-known cause. The problem is I always give but I never use the coupons. I look at the coupon booklets in my desk drawer and I think, "I should really use these." But when I scrutinize them, they really don't fit with what I eat or with how I would be purchasing - for one person. I've tried giving them away to co-workers, but they don't want them either. "Oh, no thank you," they say politely, but deep down inside I know what they are thinking. "She took them, let her deal with them."

A couple of weeks ago, I was getting a salad at one such establishment when the young man at the register asked me if I wanted to donate $1 and get a booklet with coupons worth $20. I pictured all the coupon booklets already in my possession and I thought, "This is simple. Give the donation but decline the booklet. Brilliant!" Giving makes me feel good but the coupons just make me feel guilty. I pray for the day when they expire so that I can dispose of them. Every time I open my desk drawer they stare out at me as if to say, "You are so irresponsible wasting the $1 you spent to purchase me." I hate them.

And so, I said pleasantly to the young man at the register, "I'll be glad to give a dollar, but I really don't want the coupon booklet." He stared at me, speechless, as if I was totally out of my mind, so I repeated myself. "I'll be glad to donate a dollar, but I don't want the booklet." "But it goes with the dollar," he insisted as if I didn't understand that. "I know," I said. "But I don't want to take it" "But it's free," he replied. "But I never use them," I responded. Again, he stared at me incredulously. "They make me feel guilty. I hate them," I explained hoping he would back off. "But..." he began again, at which point I raised my hand into the "stop" position. "I'm not taking them," I said firmly and evenly as I stared back at him.

As I got in my car to go back to the office I felt victorious. I had a donated a dollar, I did not have another coupon booklet to weigh on my conscience and I had a salad for lunch. I realized, however, that my hatred of the coupon booklet had grown exponentially because of my exchange with the young man at the register. When I got back to the office, before sitting down to enjoy my lunch, I flung open my top desk drawer and hurled every assorted coupon booklet into the trash can by my desk. I didn't check expiration dates. I didn't leaf through them to determine if I would ever on any occasion use one of them. I didn't even check to see where they were from. "There," I said out loud. I peered into the trash can and began shouting at them, "No more guilt from you guys! No more seeing your ugly little faces looking at me making me feel bad. I'm finished with you, I tell you. Finished. Done. Over."

I was enjoying my tirade when a co-worker interrupted as she walked past my office and observed me yelling into the trash can. "Are you okay?" she asked. "Okay?" I replied. "Okay? I'm more than okay. I'm free at last." And with that I plunged my fork into my full-price, non-bargain salad and totally enjoyed every bite.

An Extremely Dangerous Piece of Lint

17: Six Luxury Condominiums

I've been passing by a newly erected building on my way to work every day during its construction. Yesterday a sign went up. "Six Luxury Condominiums" it said in big red letters. Luxury condos, I thought. Six of them? Judging from the size of the building I doubted any one of them could offer much over 900 square feet of living space. Luxury? Limited parking. Busy street. No yard space to speak of. Luxury, really? Six of them? Well, I guess they couldn't advertise "Six Seriously Small Poorly Located Condos" on their sign in big red letters. Clearly my concept of luxury has to do with spaciousness and location.

That night when I got home I promptly consulted my "authoritative, trustworthy, current and comprehensive" American Heritage Dictionary of the English Language (Richly Illustrated in Full Color). It said:

Luxury (n.): 1. Something inessential but conducive to pleasure and comfort. 2. Something expensive or hard to obtain. 3. Sumptuous living or surroundings.

Sumptuous (adj.): Of a size or splendor suggesting great expense.

My first thought was, "Excellent! My authoritative,

trustworthy, current and comprehensive dictionary clearly agrees with my perceptions about space and luxury going hand in hand." But then I thought, "Wait a minute; everything in the definition of luxury is subjective and relative." Everything – essential vs. non-essential, what constitutes or creates pleasure and comfort, what's expensive, what's hard to obtain, even what constitutes spaciousness – all depends on where you're coming from.

Let's take my own condo as an example. My condo, I assure you, built here in coastal Massachusetts in 2001, has never been described as luxury housing. The ad for my unit could have read, "3 (extremely small) bedroom condo right next to Vinnie & Tony's Auto body shop, modular construction with the least expensive appliances, flooring and countertops along with other cheap finishing touches." When I first told a friend I was going to look at the condo, her response was, "I wouldn't look at anything on that street."

But think about it. For some families living in other parts of the world or even for some living in the United States for that matter, my condo would seem huge. The rooms are all small but if you include the finished basement, I have about 1400 square feet of living space. To a family with no indoor plumbing or running water my bath and a half, both the size of phone booths, would be a godsend. To a family living with drug lords and gang violence on the streets, being next to Vinnie and Tony, who are very nice guys and did excellent work on my car when it was rear-ended, would be a relief. My condo wasn't expensive by Massachusetts cost-of-living standards, but it was still more than a lot of people could afford. What is luxury, really?

50

Personally, I love my condo. I've made quite a few improvements. I love the location. I like the people who live next to me. I love being within a two-block walking distance of Gloucester Harbor and the shops and restaurants on Main and Rogers streets. I love my small private outside space for a deck and perennial garden. I feel safe here. It's way more than enough space for one person and two cats.

Eventually there will come the day when I sell my unit. When I do, I think I'll insist on having it listed as a "luxury" condo. It might take a while to find a realtor willing to list it as such. But in my mind, I do live in luxury. I don't care what anybody says, I live in a luxury condominium.

And so tomorrow when I pass by the Six Luxury Condominiums on my way to work, I will not pass judgment on them as I had so errantly done the day before. They may be luxury condos – or not. It all depends on who ends up living there.

An Extremely Dangerous Piece of Lint

18: A Little Abuse

There are those of us who have suffered a little abuse and there are those of us who have suffered a lifetime. There are those of us who ran as fast and far from abusive relationships as we could and there are those of us who were trapped for so long that any other form of "affection" became foreign to us.

Do any of us remember – those of us who ran and those of us who couldn't - when it began? There had to be the first time we were minimized, degraded, objectified, shoved, smacked, belittled, intimidated. It started somewhere – those first words spoken that were intended to crush our spirits. When did that first sentence occur? At birth – as an infant – a toddler – a teenager? There was a first act of physical violence – a shove, a hit, an object thrown at us. When did it start?

I suspect for most of us it began before we had any way to interpret the abuse other than that it was normal or that it was our fault. That's the thing – when it all begins, you don't know how to conceptualize it. How could you? How you could do anything other than assume that you were somehow to blame?

Here's one of the interesting things about abuse: There are those of us who have suffered a lot of abuse and, somehow, we're reasonably functioning human beings. And there are those of us who have suffered a "little abuse" and we experience its damaging effects on a daily basis. I believe this: how one reacts to abuse is not for anyone to judge and abuse is not something that can be measured. The fact is, any abuse, from a verbal put-down to a physical beating, should not be tolerated because any abuse – a little, a lot, a moderate amount – is all made of the same stuff. It's all intended to keep one powerful and one powerless, to build up the ego of one and by necessity beat down the ego of the other. The fact is, any abuse – a little, a lot, a moderate amount – compromises our ability to enter in to loving relationships and robs us of life's energy.

There's really no such thing as a little abuse because a "little" abuse can go a long way.

19: Crossing Over

I was out for a walk one evening a couple of weeks ago when I spotted an abandoned shopping cart by the side of the road a couple of blocks from the Walgreens plaza in Gloucester. I assumed it was a Walgreens cart and thought that being the helpful person I try to be I would rescue the cart and return him to his proper home. To my surprise, yet underscoring the fact that assumptions are meant to be questioned, it was a Market Basket cart. Without detailing the geography, suffice it to say, Mr. Cart was a long, long way from home. Of course, I was quite curious about how he got there. I think he would have needed to go down the highway to get here unless someone transported him in a vehicle which seemed unlikely. I figured the logical thing to do was to ask. I approached the cart and said out loud with both awe and concern, "How did you get here?" I could tell right away that he was a stoic cart, unwilling or unable to speak the truth of his situation. "You're a long way from home buddy," I said compassionately. "I was going to take you back where you belong but I'm not sure how I'd get you all the way back to Market Basket. I'm really sorry."

As I was about to apologize further I noticed a human coming down the sidewalk towards us. She took me by surprise because I was so engrossed in conversation. We had a split second of fearful eye contact at which point she looked down and quickly crossed to the other side of the road. I took pity on her and let her remove herself from us for a couple of blocks before I resumed our dialogue. "See," I said to the cart, "they cross over when they think you're odd. I mean just because you don't belong at Walgreens Plaza doesn't mean you shouldn't be treated with some level of respect." I continued to express my complete understanding. "Believe me, I've felt like a Market Basket cart in a Walgreens world."

The cart remained silent, no doubt still feeling reluctant to engage. At that point I wasn't sure what to do. I mean I couldn't just leave him there in the road. "Okay, well, I'm going to wheel you up and put you over with those Walgreens carts. Now I know you have a big label on your handle that says Market Basket but be proud of who you are. I bet you've hauled a whole lot more around in one day than those Walgreens carts have done in a week." I wanted to continue my pep talk with all kind of words of support and advice whirling around in my head. I wanted to tell him about being a Unitarian Universalist and about inherent worth and dignity. I wanted to tell him he'd fit right in with us being a bit different and all. But there were humans approaching again and I didn't want my new friend to experience yet another negative reaction. And so, I placed him side by side with the other carts and silently wished him well.

56

20: Enjoy

"He's living on borrowed time," the vet told me.
"Enjoy him."
What the doctor didn't know
Is that I understand more than I care to about bor-
rowed time.

It's all borrowed time.
We borrow months;
We borrow years;
We borrow decades, if we're lucky.
I've borrowed 47 years.

It wasn't the concept of borrowing time that I
needed to understand,
It was the concept of enjoyment.
"Enjoy him," she directed.
She said it with absolute authority.
No question, no options.
I was ordered to enjoy him ...
And that I have.

And what if someone ordered me
To enjoy my own borrowed piece of space and time?
No question, no options. "Enjoy."

An Extremely Dangerous Piece of Lint

What if I told people I was under doctor's orders
To not take everything so seriously?
What if enjoyment was the only option I had left?

I suppose, if so ordered,
I'd borrow today ... and I'd enjoy it;
And most likely I'd borrow tomorrow,
And I'd enjoy that too.

I've always known that I was a borrower,
But enjoy?
I wait for the command!

21: I See a Whale

I often walk on Stacy Boulevard in Gloucester, Massachusetts, a street that runs along the harbor where the famous Gloucester fisherman statue resides. In the summer the boulevard is filled with tourists as well as locals enjoying the spectacular view. The harbor is south-facing so to get to the open Atlantic by boat you need to go out to the mouth of the harbor about two miles and hang a left. Once in the open ocean you'd need to go a good twenty miles to see anything like whales or dolphins or to go deep sea fishing.

One day on my walk a group of three young boys about ten to twelve years old was looking out over the harbor when one of them exclaimed with great excitement, "Hey guys I think I see a whale." They sort of ignored him, so he became quite insistent. "No, really, I see a whale. I do! I see a whale." He pointed toward Ten Pound Island about a half-mile out. "See, there it is."

Now, I'm a Unitarian Universalist, so my belief system is such that I will give room for just about anything, but I really don't think there are whales living in Gloucester Harbor.

So, here's the situation. The kid firmly believes he saw a whale. He can only know what he knows, and he can't know what he doesn't know. In other words, he saw what looked to him like an ocean and he knows that things like whales live in the ocean. That's about the extent of his knowledge and understanding. He doesn't know that Gloucester Harbor faces south and is not open ocean and that creatures like whales live in the deep sea. Coincidentally, right after I started writing this short essay, I was out for a walk on the boulevard and a younger kid, about three or four, pointed to a rock in the harbor and exclaimed, "alligator!"

So, here's what strikes me: how often have I been one of those kids? I make assumptions. I think I know. I make proclamations. But what's true for them is true for me - I only know what I know and I can't know what I don't know. We're all at some level of knowledge and understanding. Never at the top level or we'd be some kind of omniscient god. Over the years I'm sure I've seen my share of whales and alligators.

Here's the lesson for me. Whenever I get all convinced I am totally right about something, I better back off. What I know could be miniscule and what I don't know could be enormous. I now tell myself that often – Jeri, what you know could be miniscule and what you don't know could be enormous. It's hard to even know where your knowledge and understanding fall on the continuum. That doesn't mean I shouldn't offer my opinion or my suggestion because it might be the best one for that time and place, but it doesn't mean in any way that I know the whole truth of a situation.

But back to the whales - everyone should go whale watching. Whales are beautiful creatures. They live in the deep sea and you have to travel some distance

60

out by boat into the open ocean to see one. Or at least I think so.

22: I'm Sorry, Your Honor

It would not be in anyone's best interest for me to be called as a witness in a court of law in the United States of America. If called, I can imagine this is what could happen:

The Judge:

Bailiff, call the next witness.

The Bailiff *(holding a King James Version of the Bible in front of me):*

Place your left hand on the Bible, hold up your right hand and repeat after me: I, Jeri Kroll, do solemnly swear.

Me *(tenuously placing my hand on the book before me):*

I, Jeri Kroll, do solemnly swear.

The Bailiff:

To tell the truth, the whole truth and nothing but the truth.

Me *(turning to the Judge for clarification):*

Is that the truth with a big "T" or a little "t"?

The Judge:

What are you, some kind of weirdo? What does it matter? Just repeat after the bailiff.

Me:

I'm sorry, Your Honor, but I don't believe in the truth with a big "T" and I'm not a weirdo, I'm a Unitarian Universalist.

The Judge *(rolling his eyes):*

That explains it. Go with a small "t" if you must.

Me:

Okay, I swear to tell the small truth, the whole small truth and nothing but the small truth.

The Bailiff: So help me God.

Me *(turning to the Judge apologetically):*

I'm sorry, Your Honor, but I'm not sure I believe in "God" (using my fingers to make quotation marks).

The Judge *(sternly):*

How about God with a small "g"?

Me *(shaking my head):*

No, God with a capital "G" or god with a small "g" – same thing.

Jeri Kroll

The Judge *(speaking to the Prosecuting Attorney):*

Let's just try to get through this. She really just needs to affirm that she's not knowingly lying. Proceed.

The Prosecuting Attorney *(turning to me):*

On the morning of October 11th did you witness the defendant, Mr. Patterson, (the Prosecutor gestures towards the defense table) driving his car down Rodgers St. in Gloucester, Massachusetts?

Me:

Well, on the day in question I did witness a person whom I perceived of as being male driving a car down Rodgers Street. I have no idea if the car was his. I suppose when you're driving down the highway you assume people are driving their own cars but I'm sure a fair number of them are borrowed or rented or maybe even stolen. My perception is that the person driving the car is the person sitting at the defense table, but he could be a man similar in appearance. Because I perceive of him as the same person does not mean he is. People think they know the truth when all they really know is their perception of the truth which could be distorted and may or may not coincide with reality.

An Extremely Dangerous Piece of Lint

I am about to launch into a spiel about an eye witness being the least reliable source of evidence and why that is when I glance over at the judge and note that he is holding his head between his palms. I interpret this to mean that he is trying to decide whether to simply dismiss me or have me held in contempt of court.

Really, I harbor no ill will or contempt toward the American judicial system, but if the questioning continued there would be a strong possibility (though no one can know for sure) that I would be the one to wind up in jail while all charges against the defendant would be dismissed even if he was guilty as sin.

No, it would definitely be best to leave me out of the judicial system and that's the truth!

Jeri Kroll

23: A Penny's Worth of Love

Pity, when we spend our love like money

Meting it out in miserly amounts,

Afraid of running out.

There've been times I've waited months

For a penny's worth of love.

But love isn't like money.

Love grows on trees,

And in dry cracks in the sidewalk,

And behind your eyes

Where it's not supposed to be.

Love isn't anything like money.

I can spend the very same penny

Over and over again

Adding up to far more than a dollar's worth

That's never given.

An Extremely Dangerous Piece of Lint

It's taken nearly fifty years of counting what I have

And what I never got,

To realize that I'm wealthy.

Because love isn't like money.

A penny's worth of love is all I'll ever need.

24: A Defining Moment

Fear is when you are out jogging and see a bull mastiff racing towards you while his owner is frantically jumping up and down and screaming, "Leave it!"

Courage is believing so completely that you are a lamp post that when the bull mastiff reaches you with his hot breath on your hand and his drool running down your leg, you do not move; you do not flinch; you are not human until his owner comes and pulls him off of you.

Wisdom is exercising further restraint when the only words the bull mastiff's owner says to you are, "Great reaction."

Unitarian Universalism is believing that both the bull mastiff and his owner have inherent worth and dignity even though in the moment this principle is hard to fathom.

Hope is believing that next time, I'll remember to take my freaking pepper spray.

Gratitude is having all your limbs intact when you get back home from an early-morning jog.

Discipline is going back out tomorrow morning despite rain, snow, sleet, hail, freezing temperatures, oppressive heat, high humidity, howling winds or ... bull mastiff.

An Extremely Dangerous Piece of Lint

25: Bad Hair Day

I was preparing a very important presentation for the board of directors for the company where I work. In thinking about the meeting, at one point I shot straight up in my chair and exclaimed in a panic, "Oh, God, I hope I don't have a bad hair day!" Not mind you "God, I hope my PowerPoint presentation graphs and charts are compelling." Not "God, I hope I'm able to answer questions intelligently and articulately." Not, "God, I hope they are receptive to exploring new directions." Nope – the number one fear (after the fear of public speaking) was – the fear of a bad hair day.

I have often wondered why those hairs sprouting out of the top of our heads are so incredibly important in our society. A Google search reveals that Americans spend about $38 billion dollars a year on hair care products. That's just products - that's not counting haircuts, coloring, braiding, ironing, foiling, feathering or perming or the time spent engaging in those activities.

Am I crazy or is this insane? It's hair. Some of us are born with hair that is easily manageable. Others - *not*. We get the frizzies in wet weather; we go completely flat and static-y when it's dry; grey hairs come in coarse. We are cursed. There's no way to win. If your hair is straight, curly is "in". If your hair is curly, straight is "in." It's no wonder when we're frustrated we use the phrase "pulling our hair out."

Really, imagine, those precious hairs – ripped out – horrifying!

Perhaps my objection to hair being so ridiculously important explains why I really, really don't like going to the hairdresser. True I don't have to get weighed and nobody tells me I need to floss more, but I'd almost rather go to my dentist or in for my annual physical, than to go to the hairdresser. Being in the dentist's chair is similar to being in the hairdresser's chair but with one huge difference - that chatty hygienist doesn't really expect you to engage in a conversation because you can't even if you wanted to. Not so the hairdresser. She expects you to carry your part of the conversation. She asks questions. She pauses when she talks, giving you the opportunity to comment. She pounces on any information you do give her and tries to probe more deeply.

The bottom line is that at the hairdresser's I feel like the proverbial fish out of water. I don't wear makeup. I don't get my nails done. I don't wear perfumes or use gels or sprays. I don't have children. I don't want to talk. And there's no way I'm ever going to look like my hairdresser despite her valiant attempts. Have you ever noticed that? Any hairdresser you go to wants your hair to look like hers when you leave. If she wears it puffed up and swept back, you will be puffed and swept; if she has bangs, you have bangs; if she wears it forward covering much of her face, forward it shall be. I keep telling my hairdresser that I'm just going to throw on a baseball cap and go for a run afterwards, so please don't bother with the gelling and the puffing and the spraying. But she does it anyway. She really can't help herself.

So back to the board of director's meeting. I may have a bad hair day. It's sort of a 50/50 proposition but I'll try to focus on what's in my head, not what's sprouting out of the top of it. With any luck that will be the board's focus as well.

Postscript: This happened several years ago. The board did in fact give me a vote of confidence to continue managing a subsidiary company that was losing a substantial amount of money every year when I took it over. I am happy to report that we managed to significantly turn things around – and I'm certain my hair has nothing to do with it.

An Extremely Dangerous Piece of Lint

26: Mistake #82531

What if we were required to keep track of the number of mistakes we made? I made at least four mistakes today that I know of. Merely counting the number of mistakes, however, could be misleading since not all mistakes are created equal.

For example:

There are *big*, major mistakes – like you married the wrong person or you thought   your fellow soldier was the enemy.

And then there are small, minor mistakes of very little consequence – like you took out the chicken to defrost and you were supposed to take out the hamburger.

Some mistakes are subjective – like you pursued the wrong career.
Other mistakes are very straightforward – like a spelling or mathematical error.

Some mistakes you can correct.
Other mistakes are best to just walk away from.

There are the mistakes you know you made.
But then there are the possible thousands of mistakes you are never aware of.

Some mistakes are the result of carelessness, but other mistakes happen despite our best efforts.

And what about the person who claims not to make any mistakes? What's up with that?

A lot of people seem to take pleasure in pointing out your mistakes, which seems totally unfair – making them is humiliating enough.

If we tracked our mistakes would it look like an inverted bell curve – more mistakes at the beginning and end of our life and fewer in the middle?

Would the types of mistakes people make follow some pattern? Like do most people make two major mistakes in a life time (one subjective and one objective); 850,000 minor mistakes (three-quarters of which they know they made and one-quarter of them unknown to them)? Of course, the people who think they make no mistakes would have all 850,000 in the "unknown" category, so the pattern theory probably doesn't hold.

To be honest, I'm not sure tracking one's mistakes would prove to have any benefit other than to dispel any pretense of perfection.

Although, it is comforting to know that since there are a finite number of mistakes that I will make in a lifetime, each mistake I make is one less I have ahead of me. Thursday, for example, I sent a Constant Contact e-mail blast to over 6000 subscribers about a seminar we're sponsoring and forgot to include the date ...Mistake #82531 – done!

27: Three Cat Poems

i.   *Jacob*

Jacob:
>loving
>loyal
>playful

>discriminating taste
>a pursuer of things in motion
>wonderfully warm and soft

>bright blue eyes
>smooth Siamese coat
>sensitive to my voice and touch a
>and presence.

Jacob:
>my buddy
>my friend
>my cat.

ii.   *The New Guys*

Shedders of paper
Climbers of curtains
Already accomplished acrobats

Loving
Alert
Loquacious

Deep blue eyes
Silky Siamese coats
10 weeks old

Benjamin
and Simon:
The New Guys

iii.   Living in the Meow

My cats do it right

No looking back
No worries about the future
No giant egos

Open to love
Eager to play
Drawn to the sun

Accepting their human
Purring their mantras
Living in the meow

An Extremely Dangerous Piece of Lint

28: Stabilization

Our maturity level at the office where I work is usually at about the junior high school level. It's not surprising, therefore, that one day we found ourselves talking about boobs – as in women's breasts. I'm not sure how it came up, but we were discussing the fact that one of the more well-endowed women we work with has often expressed disdain when others' eyes immediately focus on her chest. I know this will sound horrible. I am reviewing this writing in the wake of sexual misconduct charges running rampant in our country and the powerful "Me Too" movement. I am a woman. I support women. Sexual harassment is *never* okay. However, the well-endowed woman in our office wears such skin-tight, low-cut blouses with industrial strength under-wire bras that her breasts precede her into the room. There's just no way to not look at them. Whether you're male or female, gay or straight, attracted by them or could care less, your eyes just go there. My side comment was that I always wear a sports bra these days. "I mean it's not like I'm trying to show them off," I declared. "I'm just trying to stabilize those puppies."

Later that night at home, when my maturity level rose to near adulthood, I realized that my declaration about my own breasts was profound. That's what I've done my whole life. It's never been about showing off. It's always been about stabilization. I repeated the revelation slowly, out loud. "Never about showing off; always about stabilization." Sad, I thought. I suddenly wished I was back at the office joking around.

I knew that I could spend the remainder of the evening drumming up a lot of really, really bad memories explaining my need for safety and feeling even more and more sad, but I decided to pass on that. I've done my time in therapy, thank you very much. At this point it's all about how to move in just a little bit different direction. For me it has always been: play it safe; keep a low profile; be seen but not heard; don't rock the boat. Moving in a different direction would mean taking some risks even if they're little ones; being seen and heard; consider rocking the god-damn boat when it's called for. I'm not talking about anything big and dramatic – just something that moves me little bit outside my safety zone.

Stability, of course, isn't necessarily a bad thing. My need for safety has actually served me rather well. But when all is said and done, I hope my life will not have been exclusively about shielding myself from real or imagined harm. I think there is hope for me. I'll never be a show off, but I think I can take a risk here and there. "Cheer up," I thought. "After all, you do go bra-less as often as you can get away with it."

29: Lies

"You're stupid," my father used to say.
I can hear his voice:
>   The tone
>   The disgust
>   The finality of the conclusion.

I believed him
With the unquestioning faith of a child.
I believed I was stupid.

The lie has divided me right down the middle of my
off-centeredness.

"You'll never amount to anything," my mother
said.
I can see her face:
>   The hopelessness in her eyes
>   The disappointment
>   A certain resentment.

I believed her.
Wholeheartedly, as a child believes what a parent
says is true
I believed that I was worthless

An Extremely Dangerous Piece of Lint

The lie has divided me right down the middle of my off-centeredness.

That I now call them lies means hope.
That they divide me means work.
That I relentlessly persist in defining myself is my odyssey.

30: Religion at Its Worst

Earthquake – Haiti – 2010 - Horrific

They had prayed that their daughter would be found alive and she was! Amid shouts from the father that "God is great" the mother told reporters that they were people of faith. "Prayer really does work," she pronounced. Because this young woman was in Haiti doing volunteer relief work through a South Florida college, it was only right that she should be among those spared.

The next day different news arrived. There had been a terrible mistake. The young woman pulled from the wreckage was someone else's daughter. I wondered what pronouncements the distraught parents were now making. The father was filmed pleading with President Obama, "father to father", to please send help. I did not see the mother interviewed again. It has been eight days now since the earthquake and their daughter and thousands, yes thousands of other daughters and sons, mothers and fathers, husbands and wives have not yet been recovered. Bodies line the streets. Make shift hospitals treat the critically injured who are not necessarily the lucky ones. God is great? Prayer really does work? Really?

And then there's Pat Robertson, evangelical Christian minister, who pronounced that the people of Haiti had brought this on themselves by making a pact with the devil in order to overthrow the French. "True story," he said. I can't believe anybody buys that whole line of thinking anymore.

The problem, as I see it, is that we human beings have some innate need to know why. We want explanations. Why is there evil in the world? Why are we here? How do we know what's real? Why is one person spared and another struck down? Why? We must know why. And so we go about constructing religions and philosophies and world views to explain it all. We have prophets and saviors and religious leaders who keep us up to date if anything changes. I have nothing against religion. In fact, I would probably be considered religious. I go to church every Sunday (well, except in the summer since I'm a Unitarian), but I believe when we try to interpret events such as the earthquake in Haiti through the lens of religion, we get religion at its worst. We need to know who's responsible – the devil, the sinners who made that pact, the overpopulation, the builders, the government, the scientists who should have predicted this. "Religious" people start blaming other people because in the end it can't be the God they worship who is to blame unless of course, the people made him justifiably angry in the first place. Only the insurance companies really feel free to blame God – doesn't matter what other factors are involved, those acts of God are not covered under your policy.

Maybe it would be better to let go of that need to know why. Maybe life would actually make more sense without a neatly wrapped explanation of God, man and the universe. It would definitely be more humane. I can't image being an ordinary citizen in Haiti who has lost my family, my home, all of my possessions sitting in the rumble, smelling the stench of dead bodies and hearing the cries of those still trapped or critically injured and having some-one tell me it's my fault – because I didn't pray enough, I didn't have enough faith, I was a descend-ent of pagans.

I hope the Christian couple whose daughter was do-ing relief work gets their miracle. I really do. I hope somehow she is found alive and in one piece so that they can rejoice again with refrains of "God is great and prayer really does work". But I also hope that the atheist parents and the couple who practice voodoo and the people who never prayed at all, re-ceive a miracle too. I don't know what they would be shouting in celebration, but I hope it would not im-ply that those who did not receive the miracle are less worthy.

31: Run, Jeri, Run

My colleagues at work come from a wide geographic
area. The fact that our director of human resources
(my former boss) moved from Pennsylvania and
wound up living in the same town as I live in was a
stroke of ... well, very bad luck! We all know there
are givers and there are takers in this world – some
with a nice balance of give and take. Karen was
110% taker and 0% giver. Since she had few con-
nections with anyone in the community (no big
surprise there), whenever she needed assistance
from another human she would call on me to help.
There were the usual things we all ask people to do
for us from time to time – a ride to and from a car
dealership or a medical appointment, taking in the
mail, feeding the cat – but then there was stacking
wood in her garage when she was injured in a skiing
accident, stopping to pick up apples for her at
Brooksby Farm, getting the Christmas tree into the
house and placed in the stand and oh, yes since I
was there anyway, why not string those pesky
lights.

Then there was the time she had me drive across
town to her condo to record Dancing with the Stars
because she forgot to set it up on her DVR before
going out of town. Or the time she left her car at the
T-station when she flew back to Pennsylvania and
on the way back home realized she didn't have her
keys. She thought she might have dropped them by
her vehicle when getting out her luggage, so I drove

fifteen miles to the parking garage to look around her car for the missing keys. Not finding them there, I went into the T-station, got the number for their lost and found, located her keys, then called her back to let her know where she could, conveniently for her thank God, pick them up at a T-station on her way back from the airport.

The following incident is my favorite. One Friday morning the phone was ringing as I had one foot out the door, so I listened as it went to voicemail. It was Karen asking if I would go to her condo and get her passport. She was in Vermont for work and had decided to go from there up to Canada for a weekend of skiing. I was to overnight her passport to her sister's house, so she'd be able to pick it up on Saturday morning. She left the address on the voicemail but oh, she didn't know the zip code, so I'd have to find that out. I stared at the answering machine for a moment and then, shaking my head stated slowly and deliberately, "No. Nope. I've had enough. I've done enough. I'm going to pretend I already left for work. I never got the message." I gathered my stuff and rushed to the car muttering, "You already left for work. You never got the message. You already left for work. You never got the message."

Once in the car, however, I thought things like, "What if *you* were all alone? What if *you* had nobody and *you* needed help? And what about the UU principle of treating everyone (even Karen) with dignity and respect?" "Alright", I sighed, rubbing my forehead as I trudged back into the house to write down the address. As I re-played the message, however, it struck me again how many things she assumed I would do for her. I think it was the needing to

90

find out the zip code that got me. "No", I com-
manded myself out loud. "You're not doing it." I
forced myself back into the car without writing
down the information.

This time I got as far as starting my vehicle when I
thought, "Oh, no, what if I'm in a horrible car accident which I would have avoided if I'd taken the time
to go get the fucking passport?" I thought of one of
my favorite movies, Run, Lola, Run, in which the
same scenario is played out three times with dras-
tically different results depending on seemingly
small decisions. Several trips in and out of the
house later, I sat in the car with address in hand
and thought to myself, "This is when being a UU has
its draw backs. I mean if I was a Christian I could
have asked myself twenty minutes ago, 'What would
Jesus do?'" But then I thought, "Oh, no. I'm pretty
sure Jesus would have said, 'fuck that bitch.'"

In the end I drove to Karen's condo and found her
passport – not easy since it wasn't exactly where
she said it would be, of course. I thought it might
save time in the long run if I went ahead and fed the
cat, changed the litter box, set up the DVR, brought
in the mail, stacked the wood, stocked her fridge
with apples and hung some holiday decorations but
then I'd be really late for work. So, having retrieved
the passport I drove to work *accident-free* where I
had a phone message from Karen. "Never mind,"
she said, half-laughing. "I decided not to go skiing
this weekend after all." I figured it was safe to para-
phrase what Jesus himself had said earlier that
morning and exclaimed, "What ... a ... bitch."

32: The Web

For about a month now I have been reading the Unitarian Universalist principles out loud in the morning as part of a meditation of sorts. My goal has been to embrace a more positive attitude toward humanity since often times to me people seem nothing more than a source of irritation. You can see why I felt an attitude adjustment was in order. The last UU principle is to "respect the interdependent web of all existence of which we are a part." Since starting my mornings by reading the principles, I fell into the habit of declaring cheerfully as I left the house, "I'm in the web." I then focused on appreciating the world and the people around me. Things were going well until yesterday.

I had stopped after work on my way home to drop off a donation from the charitable foundation of which I am a member to a school serving disadvantaged children in our community. My interaction with the executive director who took my picture presenting the check to the chief financial officer left me feeling warm and fuzzy. When I arrived home I quickly changed into my jogging gear and headed out for a run. The streets were pretty much devoid of other people since it had started to snow rather heavily. I love running under those conditions – fighting the elements, feeling strong and solid.

As I was jogging down one of the more heavily traveled streets in town, a car pulled over and the passenger side window rolled down. The driver leaned over and asked, "Hey pal, where's the high school ice rink?" "High school?" I responded knowing that the ice rink was at the middle school not the high school. "Yes, high school," he responded in a hostile tone. "Ice rink?" I replied trying to be helpful and not send him to the wrong location. The man then leaned closer to the window so that I could see the utter contempt on his face. Still I assumed (trying to maintain that positive attitude toward humanity) that at worst he was going to say, "Yes, ice rink, you moron." Instead, he cut to the chase. "Fuck you" he spat and sped off, taking a sharp left before I could barely blink an eye.

I stood there stunned. Finally, I responded with my voice trailing off, "Oh, yeah, well fuck you too, motherfucker." I then decided a double-fisted middle-finger salute was called for and so even though he was long gone I jogged for several blocks with my fists raised and my fingers appropriately positioned. I neither noticed nor cared about what anyone else who happened to pass me by would think.

Later when I had time to reflect on the brief encounter, all I could do was shake my head. I conjured up an image of the man asking for directions and tried my Unitarian Universalist hardest to accept him into the web.

Since my initial writing about this incident, I am midway through our church's common read Cultivating Empathy – The Worth and Dignity of Every Person – Without Exception by Nathan Walker. Perhaps by the time I finish the book I'll come to terms with the fact that there are all kinds of critters in the web. But I can see where it's all heading. The question for me will be – what am I weaving?

33: The Part

I just don't have the part required

You know the one so highly desired.

Some say, "It's not its size that matters."

While others brag, "Mine's longer, fatter."

I assure you it's not the part per se,

That's envied by most of us lackers.

It's equal work for equal pay.

It's privilege, power and backers.

I'd really rather not have the part.

It's proven to steal from the conscience and heart.

But wouldn't it be great if discrimination ceased,

And the fattest of all was my salary increase!

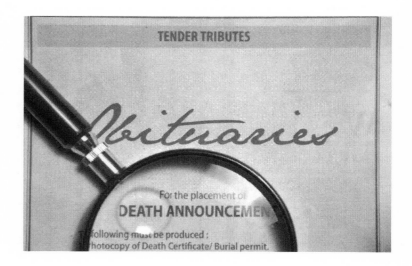

34: Obituary

I had a boss once, the director of human resources, who, whenever anybody left the department, would round all of us up to explain the shift in personnel. It was common knowledge that she had fired one of the women in the department at the beginning of the week. By mid-week, sure enough we were all summoned into a meeting where Sandy announced quite formally and as if this was good news, "I have gathered you all here today to let you know that Barbara is pursuing other opportunities." My lip curled up on one side, my eyes narrowed, and my jaw dropped slightly as I gave her my best "what the fuck" look. I managed to refrain from vocalizing the truth, "You fired her sorry ass."

On a positive note, I got to thinking that the line would make a great gravestone epitaph. "Here lies Jeri Kroll, she is pursuing other opportunities." Of course, any good UU would react the way I had about Barbara and say, "What the fuck – she's dead!"

Then I got to thinking, what will they say about me when I'm dead? Since I'm not likely to have a burial plot with a headstone I suppose all that will be left behind to describe me will be some lame obituary in a local newspaper somewhere. One of my biggest fears is that all that would be written about me is, "She was nice" or maybe "She was quiet" and now she's really quiet. Not that being nice or being quiet aren't nice but talk about B-O-R-I-N-G. To be on the safe side I should probably write my own obituary. Some people do that. I had a friend who recorded a videotape of himself that was played on a big screen in the front of the church at his funeral service. It was kind of creepy, really, because his opening words were, "Hi everybody. I'm dead."

So, if it's safer to write my own obit, the question is, how would I describe myself? I was what? What adjectives other than "nice" or "quiet" would apply? After considerable thought I really like the word "unassuming". The word would describe me on two levels. On the one level, the word does describe me according to the common definition. I quote my trusty American Heritage dictionary – "unassuming – exhibiting no pretentions, boastfulness or ostentation." Yeah, that's me. I wouldn't be particularly thrilled about the word though, if it didn't have another meaning which fits perfectly with being a Unitarian Universalist. As UU's we don't make assumptions. We don't assume we know the truth. We don't assume there is one way to practice spirituality. We're an unassuming group of people.

The problem is if I used the word "unassuming" I'm not sure how many people would get it. They'd probably equate it with "nice" and I'd be right back in the same bind.

I think the best route is to keep it simple and direct. Just say "she was a UU". Since most people don't know what that means they won't equate it with nice or quiet. Of course, I hope the need for a final decision about this matter is not imminent but for now if any of my loved ones are listening and I come to the end of the line, please don't describe me as

nice or quiet or unassuming or say that I am pursuing other opportunities. Just say, "she was a UU"
and leave it at that.

35: To Robert

(1944 – 1997)

Of all my memories

I recall most vividly

the day you learned of your diagnosis –

Tall, thin, ruggedly handsome,

Internationally renowned psychiatrist,

Arrogant, superior, fifty-two.

Your lower lip was trembling.

"I just found out I have colon cancer."

We all just sat there.

Silent.

For twelve of the thirteen months that followed

It was business as usual:

  you saw patients;

An Extremely Dangerous Piece of Lint

       we developed assessment tools;

       we spoke at conferences.

But I always found myself watching your lower lip,

Fascinated by your vulnerability,

Waiting for a second revelation of our equality.

I never witnessed the trembling again.

The lower lip remained steady, certain, determined.

Yet of all my memories of you

It was that day,

That day you learned of your diagnosis,

That I will never forget.

Jeri Kroll

35: To Wilma

(1927 – 1975)

I see your blood:

> wet

> bright red

> spilling out everywhere from your nose
> and ears and mouth.

I hear your screams:

> piercing

> angry

> desperate.

I feel the confusion of an unacceptable reality.

I see your body flopping about by the side of the
road,

your crumpled bicycle thrown in the opposite direction.

I hear sirens in the distance.

I feel the sudden intrusion of a crowd of people;

a man identifying himself as a reporter is asking
me what happened;

An Extremely Dangerous Piece of Lint

I am enraged by his stupidity.

I feel the grip of a stranger pulling me back.

I smell the spring wildflowers and grasses, the moist earth and water of the lake below.

I hear the matter-of-fact words of the nurse who stopped to help,

"It doesn't look good."

I feel the numbness of utter helplessness.

The memories of your death arrive quite uninvited,

provoked by some familiar, now unwelcome sense:

> a sight,
>
> a sound,
>
> a smell.

Images too real for the passage of time because I

> see your blood,
>
> hear your screams,
>
> feel the confusion.

37: Degrees and Certifications

I have a master of divinity degree, but I'll be honest – I rarely admit it! To begin with, "master of divinity" sounds just plain pompous. People's assumptions about you when they find out you have an MDiv can be disturbing. Some assume you are "religious" in the traditional, uncomfortable sense. Others think they need to behave differently around you like you're judging them. Some think you think you're better than they are. Anyone who knows me would hardly refer to me as divine let alone mastering the quality.

I do feel compelled to point out that obtaining a master of divinity degree is no easy feat, at least not where I earned mine – through a three year post graduate program which included becoming proficient in Greek and Hebrew. If I could insert some choice swear words from those two languages I would but I can't figure out how to get my computer to use Greek or Hebrew characters.

I suppose in some ways it's sad that I will never string a bunch of (or even one) degrees or credentials after my name. In my field of human services and education people tend to include as many as they can. Most of the time nobody knows what the hell the initials stand for or if they are even legitimate. I wonder if the inclusion of the degrees and certifications after one's name is solely for professional purposes so other people respect their qualifications or does it go deeper than that?

It seems that people who have licenses or certifications do refer to themselves as a "licensed" or a "certified" whatever indicating it is who they are. "I'm a licensed social worker or plumber or massage therapist". With educational degrees there seems to be more separation semantically but still the degree morphs into part of the person's identity – for example you wouldn't say "I'm a PsyD" but you would say, "I'm a psychologist."

Since I won't include MDiv after my name and since for most degrees people don't know what all those letters stand for anyway, I figure why not pick something that speaks to my own chosen identity. For example:

Jeri Kroll, MCRW
Master of Creative and Ridiculous Writing

I can picture myself in a meeting where professionals are introducing themselves. I would introduce myself by saying, "Hi, I'm Jeri. I have an MCRW." Everyone would nod approvingly too embarrassed to admit they didn't know what an MCRW was. In the very unlikely event someone asked about it I would respond by saying something like "Oh, you didn't know? It's a new degree they offer at UC-Berkeley". Everyone would nod again even more impressed that I had completed a new degree program at one of the country's top schools of social work. If anyone pressed me further, I guess I'd need to pretend I got an emergency call from one of my nonexistent clients.

The beauty of making up your own degree or credential is that it only takes a matter of moments to switch to a whole different career or identity.

To be serious for a moment, I believe to a large degree we can choose our own identities. Yes, there are all kinds of influences that have shaped us from the time of our birth and yes, there are genetic factors. At some point, however, hopefully we see the options that are available to us. We consciously ask ourselves, "Who am I? Who do I want to be?". We create our own string of identifying letters and abbreviations. Of course, this task is not as easy as creating those made-up identifiers which can shift in a matter of moments. The real letters take work. Sometimes the real letters are horrifying and we need to change them – which takes even more work.

As a Unitarian Universalist I strive for my real letters to reflect our principles. I could make up letters for each of the principles but maybe it's best summed up as:

Jeri Kroll, LHG
Liberal Humanitarian Globalist

How about you? What would your letters be?

"You were born an original. Don't die a copy."
John Mason

"Why try to be someone you're not. Life is hard enough without adding impersonation to the skills required.
Robert Brault

38: The Question

"Who do you think you are?" she asked me,

Each word emphasized;

Every syllable filled with disdain.

WHO DO YOU THINK YOU ARE?

Silence.

Years of silence.

Today, I hear this same question

Often hidden in a remark,

> a look,

> an attitude.

And I find myself asking the question all over
again,

As if there never had been an adequate answer all
these years.

WHO DO I THINK I AM?

An Extremely Dangerous Piece of Lint

Somebody?

Anybody?

Nobody?

In the present hearing,

I will answer that I am somebody;

not perfect,

not wonderful,

not all it was hoped I would be,

but somebody.

The answer suffices ...

for now.

39: Wham, Bam, Spam

Note: Because of my first name, I frequently receive e-mails or correspondence assuming I am male.

Yesterday our IT department confirmed that the filters designed to weed out spam are effective for a couple of months and then, bam, the spam floods your email inbox as the scammers have figured out a way to break through. A couple of months ago I started collecting a bunch of these e-mails after one such break through because an evil plot was forming in my mind. Why not respond to them with a dose of their own medicine by connecting them with each other?

Here's how it would work.

I received the following e-mail dated September 10th from Miss Joyce, 5:23 a.m.

"Dear, How are you? Am very happy to your email profile today and will like to establish a long lasting relationship with you, in addition I will like to discuss more important issue with you. Waiting for your responses, God bless you and your family. Yours Sincerely, Miss Joyce"

On September 13th I received this e-mail from Aisha Arop, at 5:26 a.m.

"Hello,
Am a young single girl never married seeking true love for a long term relationship with marriage potentials, I am happy to contact you because you cut my interest!i will love us to be good friends or a lot more, you can contact me .so that I will send you my photos,till I hear from you, bye and kisses! Miss Aisha"

It was obvious to me that these two women were perfect for each other and decided the following responses were in order:

Dear Miss Aisha,
By luck of chance I was in receipt of correspondence by Miss Joyce just three days ago. She also is seeking a long lasting relationship. God has blessed us with so many lesbians worldwide! As I am have a girlfriend already I have the most good fortune to connect you with Miss Joyce. God bless!

Dear Miss Joyce,
God works in such wonderful ways. You will with luck and God's blessing be hearing from Miss Aisha who is cut with interest in you after much prayer. As I have come to know both of you I am certain that this union of two God-fearing and holy women will be a cause for celebration in your country. God bless you both and kisses.

40: Today is the Tomorrow I Talked about Yesterday

I'm constantly having trouble with my e-mail at work. I'm located in a satellite office, so our computer system taps into the main office via our server. "Server" is definitely a misnomer.

A couple of weeks ago I had sent an e-mail to a colleague about two o'clock in the afternoon, saying "see you tomorrow" at a training we were conducting together – it was actually meant to be a friendly, gentle reminder of the date. I realized about an hour after I sent the e-mail that all my e-mails for the past several hours were stuck in my outbox and had not been sent. Our oh-so-responsive IT department was not able to assist me in correcting the situation that day but by mid-morning the next day we were back in business. What complicated matters was that all the e-mails intended to be sent the day before went out dated and timed as if I had sent them that morning when they flew into cyberspace from my outbox. My message saying, "see you tomorrow" sent my co-trainer into a panic thinking she had already driven half way to her destination on the wrong day.

By the time I was dealing with a third misunderstanding I simply explained, "today is the tomorrow I talked about yesterday." After the explanation rattled around in my head for a while, I thought, wow, that's actually meaningful. Today was tomorrow yesterday and yesterday tomorrow was today. All of which means, as we know from so many wise sources, it all circles back to the importance of today, the importance of now.

From a time management perspective rather than a spiritual one, I suppose if we all really did the things we said yesterday that we'd do today and we just went on like that day to day living on a borrowed tomorrow it would all work out okay. At the end you'd only be off by one day so hopefully that one last thing you never did was not too terribly important. The problem is that we think we have an endless supply of tomorrows but on any given day you only have one tomorrow if you're lucky and then like clockwork it's today again with just that one tomorrow.

From a more philosophical perspective, time is an odd concept. No matter what you do time just keeps coming at you – rolling through you and then behind you. You can't stop it. You can't save it, really. All you can do is make choices about how you're going to roll with it. I'm always analyzing, organizing and dissecting everything but I like the concept of rolling – it makes life sound like fun rather than all task-oriented and serious.

Rolling requires living in the now because you can't really plan to roll, you just do it. Imagine getting up in the morning and simply saying to yourself, "Okay, let's roll!" In the back of your mind of course you'd know what needed to be done that day but in the front of your mind you'd just think about rolling. I'm not sure I can roll all the time or, shit, who am I kidding, even half the time, but I'd like to.

114

Okay, so maybe I'll shoot for a sixteenth of the time ... or ... okay, well, maybe I'll just feel good that at least I can conceptualize it. But to all of you I bid, "roll on!"

41: Last Chance

About two weeks ago I received a call on my cell phone. I don't use my cell phone except for emergencies so I was panicked as I scrambled to find the annoying device. To my even greater annoyance, the call was a recorded message from my car manufacturer telling me this was my last chance to extend the warranty on my vehicle. I don't know why, but I politely listened to the whole message before I was given two options. Press "1" to talk to a representative or press "2" to be taken off the list and not contacted again. A sense of relief washed over me as I pressed "2," knowing that not only would they never call again, but nobody I loved had been killed or horribly disfigured in some ungodly accident.

About three days later my cell phone rang again and again I was panicked. Some great tragedy was finally and inevitably unfolding. But no, it was the car manufacturer again telling me this was my last chance to extend the warranty on my vehicle. I listened closely to the same recorded message trying to figure out if I had not heard it correctly the first time. This time I also heard the underlying message. The stern, business-like voice was saying, "Press '1' now you idiot because we're not going to bother to call someone as stupid as you again. If you are dumb enough to press '2,' that piece of crap you call a car will fall apart within a week and that will be what you deserve".

As I continued to listen, I realized that I had in fact taken in the information correctly. It was my last chance. If I did not press "1," I would lose the only chance I would ever be given to extend my warranty. I was also correct in hearing that if I pressed "2," I would not under any circumstances, no matter how sorry I was for my decision, be contacted again. This time I was not relieved, I was pissed off. Perhaps I had not pressed "2" with enough force the first time, so I stabbed an angry finger into the number "2" on the keypad and shouted some choice expletives into the phone for good measure.

Three days later – yep, another last chance. This time I decided it was all good. To my amazement, in just a couple of calls I had already become desensitized to the ring of the cell phone. I no longer swerved off the road or tossed all my belongings out of my bag in a frantic attempt to find the devise. I no longer envisioned myself rushing to a hospital emergency room to hear my partner's dying words. I was more mature, my outlook more positive. Life was better now. When the cell phone rang my thoughts could be, "Oh, yes, nobody's dead or maimed, just a telemarketer." Light, breezy thoughts. Really, I should thank the car manufacturer for their persistence. Why had I sworn at them several days ago? Obviously, they had done more to improve my mental health than years of therapy had managed to accomplish.

More than that, the car manufacturer had assisted me in re-assessing my approach to life. When you think about it, there aren't that many true last chances. Maybe shortly before I'm dead there will be a few but other than that it seems to me there's an endless stream of possibilities and opportunities and alternatives. It's more like having a different

118

chance, not a last chance. Salespeople are into the "last chance" mentality but frankly I don't want my life driven by the fear that I'm going to lose out. Maybe it's the aging thing, as I am about to turn sixty, but it seems important for me to abandon all traces of that "last chance" mentality and see my future as full of all sorts of possibilities.

Two nights ago when I arrived home there, was a message on my answering machine. It was my telephone carrier telling me it was, yes, my last chance to sign up for a great new service plan. This time I was not at all annoyed by the call. Instead, I smiled, wondered how many more times they would leave the same message, and thought about my resolve to abandon the "last chance" mentality.

An Extremely Dangerous Piece of Lint

42: Just Another WTF Moment

It was the winter of 2015 in Boston, Massachusetts, mid-March and it was already record breaking:

Snowiest winter on record
Snowiest February on record
Most sub-freezing days in February on record
Two of the top ten heaviest snowstorms on record

North of Boston where I live conditions were even worse. Although I am not aware of any specific records documenting this, Gloucester, according to the local meteorologists was always in the "jackpot zone" for snowfall. There were also no records documenting the amount of stress we endured. Driving around our cities and towns turned beyond hazardous. Vehicles lurched out in front of you from snow banked side roads. Two-way streets had barely one passable lane. The constant slamming into potholes you never saw coming was unnerving. For at least a good two months in my community, there were no sidewalks cleared for pedestrians or for those like me who exercise by walking.

I thought about joining a gym but ruled that out for a number of reasons. Having gotten to the point of desperation, I decided to try something I never dreamed I would ever consider – mall walking.

I have to admit, mall walking proved to be much better exercise than I gave it credit for. But here was the problem, after a couple of trips to the mall entering through the Macy's petite section where everything was attractively displayed and on sale, I entered the mall the third time sans sneakers, with credit card. I mean seriously, I needed larger-sized slacks because I was down to only two pairs that fit me. As I placed my three new pairs of pants on the checkout counter, the cashier asked me cheerfully if I would be using my Macy's credit card today. When I responded that I would not be, she asked pleasantly if I wanted to apply for one which would only take a few moments. For some reason, I blurted out honestly, "Oh I probably have one. I get them when there's a special deal and then I cut them up.

"Oh," she snarled as her friendly smile immediately turned to a scowl. In hindsight I think it was the "cutting up" that had a rather negative effect. Perhaps if I'd said meekly, "I don't usually end up using them," it might have been more palatable. The clerk silently proceeded to process my purchase, snatched my Amazon credit card from my hand and printed out the receipt. As she handed me the copy I needed to sign she stated with no affect, "So, you got a 10% discount because you used a card other than Macy's today." Wait. Did she say what I think she just said? Didn't she just try to get me to open a Macy's account and then I would have paid more? Really? I must be mistaken. I glanced quickly at my receipt, which verified I had in fact received a 10% discount. I stood there speechless until the customer behind me started nudging me out of the way.

As I exited the store into the parking lot it seemed to me that there were so many ways to think about the encounter. Miraculously, the question that rose to the top of my brain was "Why must I analyze everything to death? Why am I such a classic overthinker? Why can't I just mutter, 'What the fuck' and be done with it?"

I decided there was no time like the present to try out this revolutionary "what the fuck" practice. As I closed the car door, I shook my head and said aloud, "Oh well, just another WTF moment." It's the new me!

An Extremely Dangerous Piece of Lint

"Some flies and gnats were sitting on my paper and this disturbed me; I breathed on them to make them go, then blew harder and harder, but it did no good. The tiny beasts lowered their behinds, made themselves heavy, and struggled against the wind until their tiny legs were bent. They were absolutely not going to leave the place. They would always find something to get hold of, bracing their heels against a comma or an unevenness in the paper, and they intended to stay exactly where they were until they themselves decided it was the right time to go."

Knut Hamsun

124

43: Bug on the Windshield

I noticed the bug on the outside of my windshield when I started up my vehicle. He was varying shades of brown, about two inches long with wings, a bunch of legs and two antennae. Some sort of beetle I guessed. I call him a "he" but he could just as easily have been a "she." I'd like to think gender doesn't matter so much anymore. I considered getting out of the car and shooing him off the windshield before I drove off, but I figured he'd take flight soon after I started moving. Boy was I wrong.

At first everything was fine. The bug rode along as if he was an invited guest. But in no time at all he looked like a palm tree in a category five hurricane. How could he possibly hold on like that? Soon I would be on a major highway and I figured that would spell disaster for the hapless insect. I began imploring him to let go. "Let go bug, just let go" I chanted. "Let go." But, no – the bug was clinging on for dear life.

Upon entering the highway, I was horrified when the bug started losing body parts. "Let go," I screamed – no more gentle chanting. But the more I screamed the more fiercely he held on. Another limb was ripped off. "Just let go," I screamed again as I took both hands off the wheel and gestured toward him. Maybe he didn't understand English but surely, he should understand the universal sign for "go." When it was obvious my screaming and gestures were to no avail I decided I had no choice and pulled off the highway at the next exit. I was hoping of course that when I stopped the bug would think, "Oh, thank God, I will now fly away to safety." But no, that little motherfucker refused to let go.

I sat there exasperated. The reality is I'm a complete wuss when it comes to insects. Getting within arm's length of anything that has wings, a bunch of legs and two antennae requires a kind of courage I'd rather not summon up unless it's a really, really special occasion. So, I sat there a bit longer, hoping I did not have the dumbest bug in the world on my windshield and that he would ultimately see the wisdom in taking off. But no, no such luck.

Again, there didn't seem to be much choice. I had to get out of the car and manually remove him. "But maybe he's too damaged to save," I thought hopefully. I scooted over closer to his side of the windshield to assess the situation. It looked like one antenna and maybe two legs were lost but the other antenna was moving around and his wings were sort of twitching. He looked salvageable. Since he was moving a bit I thought maybe he would end up taking off on his own accord. Maybe I just needed to be more patient. I considered turning on the windshield wipers to dislodge him but ruled that out as potentially counterproductive not to mention messy. I waited about ten minutes longer and well, as you might guess, the little asshole just sat there twitching.

"Okay," I told myself. "You can do this." I searched around in the car for an envelope or heavy piece of paper for maneuvering him off the windshield. Eventually I found an empty manila folder that seemed like a viable tool. I got out of my vehicle and

126

approached the bug cautiously. "I hope you appreciate this" I muttered. Apparently, he did not appreciate it because he adamantly refused to get on the damn folder. Every time I thought I had him on it, he'd manage somehow to maneuver himself off. I couldn't bear the thought of driving off again and leaving him there to be torn apart limb by limb. "This is for your own good," I told him as I persisted in my mission to dislodge my small, ugly, obstinate friend from my car. Finally, somehow, I got him on the manila folder and carried him into a small wooded area of birch trees nearby. Once again, I underestimated his tenacious character. Now he would not get off the fucking folder. I shook it. I waved it. I blew on it. I jumped up and down making bird noises. I called him every bad name I could think of, which felt really good, but clearly, he was not moving.

Finally, I put the folder down on the ground. "You are one stubborn bastard," I declared, pointing a finger at him. His one remaining antenna snapped up in a salute of sorts. I interpreted it to mean, "Damn straight chickie." I decided I didn't really need the manila folder and if left there it would disintegrate without any serious harm to the environment. I mean, why pit my will any further against a being with whom I was clearly not an equal? "Okay bug, well good luck," I said.

A few days later as I thought about the incident, I decided that the bug really needed an insect's version of the Serenity Prayer which, actually, in some circumstances might be good for us humans too.

An Extremely Dangerous Piece of Lint

God grant me the serenity to let go when I would otherwise be ripped apart;

The courage to hold on for dear life when that's what is required;

And the wisdom to know the difference.

Jeri Kroll

44: The Most Important Day of My Life

Quite a while ago I entered an essay contest in which the writer was tasked with describing the most important day of his or her life. Examples of prior winning entries included descriptions of a couple's wedding day, a birth, a graduation, and so on. Granted the pieces were extremely well- written, but frankly, I thought the topic was utterly stupid!

The most important day of my life, of course, would have to be the one I'm in. How could it be otherwise? If the most important day of my life is not the one I have before me or in other words the most important day of my life has already passed such that I could point to a specific day and say, "That's it; that's the day," what does that say about my life going forward? Wouldn't the rest of my days be rather anti-climactic, at best?

I suppose I could have another most important day of my life and then another and then another depending on how long I live. But then how could one judge whether or not that next best day was actually more important than the previous best day?

Perhaps the more significant question would be, what would make one day more important than another? Would it depend on how I felt about it or how I thought about it from my limited perspective or is there some higher being who would determine that?

If a higher power determined which day was the most important, then I wouldn't be able to point to the day myself and say, "Aha, that's my most important day." If I did try to make that determination, maybe I'd be completely and utterly wrong. Maybe what I thought was a wonderful day actually set into motion a tragic event or even a tragic series of events.

Mrs. Nelson, my eighth grade English teacher, said that one should not end a sentence with a preposition. But the most important day of my life should be the one I'm in.

This day – the one I'm in, Mrs. Nelson, is all I really have.

45: The Wonderful, Magnificent Blue Bike

For more than a decade now I have been accompanying my partner, Jodi, to Hilton Head Island, South Carolina at Christmas time to visit her parents who live in one of the many gated communities built around the greens and fairways of eighteen-hole golf courses. A labyrinth of bike paths that weave in and out of picturesque lagoons and harbors make bike riding one of our favorite activities when we're there.

Jodi's father, now in his eighties, grew up in the Great Depression and worked his way up from blue collar beginnings to an executive position with General Electric. Predictably, he has difficulty throwing anything away or spending his money on anything new if it can be purchased second hand. This includes his clothing which quite frankly often makes him look like a homeless person. Twice a week Jodi's dad works at a thrift shop called the Bargain Box fixing electrical items that come in. One of the benefits of working at the Bargain Box is that he often has first dibs on the merchandise. His collection of used bicycles is an example of this "advantage."

While in Hilton Head for the holidays, I have always been assigned one particular bicycle in the fleet – the "wonderful, magnificent blue bike." The blue bike is probably a kid's bike. It's small, baby blue where not rusted out, with a seat similar in cushioning to a cinder block – single speed. The word "speed" is a misnomer as is the term "brakes." Pedaling the blue bike which makes a constant high-pitched squealing sound as if it is being tortured takes an excruciating amount of effort. Even on a level surface coercing the blue bike forward takes a tremendous amount of muscle power. The other bikes in the fleet are also used but actually in fairly good shape. All of them have at least several speeds and seem eager to move forward effortlessly and without complaint.

Every year the blue bike and I began to fall further and further behind the others. In the early years I tried my hardest to keep up. In my family and Jodi's there had always been an emphasis on physical fitness. It was not acceptable to be the weakest, the least fit, the one who came in last. And so, I pushed myself relentlessly. I might have been too winded to talk, and my muscles might have been burning so badly I'd hobble around when we stopped to do a little sightseeing, but I tried. One year I made the decision to stop trying. "Let them go," I said to myself. "Let's face it. You're probably just plain last-place material."

In fairness to Jodi, she would suggest from time to time that we switch bikes. I always declined the offer, partly because the other bikes were too big for me but mainly because I feared she would take off effortlessly on the blue bike, unhindered by its flaws. If that were to happen I would be horrified. I would know for certain that it was not the bike that was flawed but me. And so, the blue bike and I stuck together both of us secretly wondering which one of us was to blame.

132

Harbor Town, which is within the Sea Pines Plantation where Jodi's parents live, has been one of our usual biking destinations. There are quaint shops, restaurants, tennis courts, luxury condos and huge yachts docked there from as far away as the Marshall Islands. I always think we look like a band of bicycled misfits as we pedal into the village. One year, because the blue bike was also difficult to steer, I got tangled up in the ropes lining the harbor walk and ended up with the bike dangling dangerously toward the water while I clung to the ropes. Fortunately, we were extricated by the others who eventually noticed we were missing. That was probably our worst moment together.

Last week Jodi went to Hilton Head without me. Her sister and brother, along with his new girlfriend, made the early spring trip to deal with some aging parent issues that many of us baby boomers have in common. It didn't dawn on me until later that if bike riding was part of the agenda for the large contingent of visitors, someone else would have to ride the blue bike. Jodi arrived late at night and called me the next evening for a status report. We chatted for about half an hour, mainly discussing how her parents were doing. About fifteen minutes after we hung up, the phone rang. It was Jodi. "Just one more thing," she announced in a serious tone. "My God," I thought. "What could it be?" "The blue bike," she said. "I am so, so very, very sorry. For all the times ..." she started to say but trailed off as we both started laughing. "So," I thought, "Jodi was the lucky one?" "Apology accepted," I told her.

After we hung up I sat down feeling amused but also extremely fortunate. How many of us ever get a real apology? Most often when someone says, "Oh, gee, I'm sorry" he or she is really saying "okay, let's move along now and forget about what happened." The apology has nothing to do with you. It's all about the other person's need to feel okay with him or herself again.

Sometimes people use "I'm sorry" to justify an action before they do it. For example, at work often times someone will say, "I'm sorry to interrupt" but it's clear they totally intend to interrupt and are not sorry at all.

I suppose there are all sorts of apologies in all sorts of contexts but if someone offers you an apology it should definitely be about you. A real apology should have an element of, "I understand the impact of my actions from your point of view." That night I received a real "I'm sorry" from Jodi.

But perhaps the best part of the apology is that it resulted in this: my blue bike days are over! Not that I won't ever again ride the blue bike, who now seems more like an old friend than my arch-enemy, but when I do, I will never, ever again entertain the thought that I'm just plain last-place material.

134

46: I'm Not Here. Can I Take a Message?

It's my standard response to an unknown caller asking to speak to me. "She's not here; can I take a message?" I try to say this quite pleasantly so as not to tip off the caller that I'm a lying sack of shit. Despite my best efforts, there are times I can tell the caller knows I'm lying. There's a pause and an awkward "oh" followed by another long pause. At that point I'm tempted to say, "Oh, okay, alright, you win, it's me," but I never do. Of course, no-one has ever confronted me on it. I mean, saying "I know it's you, you worthless, piece of crap", probably wouldn't be a good way to get me to buy a product or give my money away. And so, the caller, who also needs to maintain the charade, asks pleasantly, "When would be a good time to catch her?"

Now there's a legitimate question! When would be a good time to catch me? I have no answer for that. It does make me wonder what I might be missing by being so protective of myself. Maybe the caller is going to tell me I've won the Publishers Clearing House Sweepstakes and they need to arrange a time to arrive at my house to film me all ecstatic in my bathrobe.

Seriously, what might I be missing? When meeting a new person do I immediately shut him or her out by not being there? Probably. What opportunities have I missed? What ideas and energy and relationships and serendipitous moments have I side stepped? God only knows, but I'm certain it would be a lot.

When all is said and done, I suppose I need to make a decision. How open will I or can I be to the unknown? I have to admit it does sound appealing on some level to be able to say, "Hey, I'm here. This is me." I can say "no" to you or I can say "yes" to you. I can say "yes" now and then say "no" later. I don't need to please you. I don't need to protect you. The only requirement is that I respect you and you respect me. How damned hard is that? As with most of this shit, it's a whole lot harder and more complicated than it sounds.

I do believe I will try to move in that direction. But, in the meantime, I'm calling the phone company to order caller ID as soon as possible!

Jeri Kroll

47: Say "Yes" If You Want to Leave a Call-back Number

Last week I was following up on the task of applying for Medicare. I'm turning sixty-five and was advised to apply even if I intended to continue working. I had decided to call the Social Security Administration office rather than file on line or send in an application because my brother (who is a lot smarter than I am) said he made a mistake when he filed so I figured I should play it safe and have a live person walk me through the process.

I called the number for the Social Security office and was greeted, of course, by an automated voice giving me options. I answered with the appropriate "yes" and "no" responses until finally, some ten minutes later, I got to the extension I needed. At that point the automated voice instructed me that I could either say "yes" if I wanted to leave a call-back number or stay on the line and wait forty-two minutes to talk to someone. Without giving it a thought, I blurted out, "Jesus fucking Christ – forty-two minutes?" Since I was at work the call-back option wasn't feasible, so I started to settle in to wait as long as I could. To my surprise, however, the automated voice came back on the phone immediately and said patronizingly, "Okay then, let's start again." I held the phone away from my ear and looked at it in horror. I was just supposed to stay on the line. My outburst was merely my own private expression of exasperation. Surely even a machine

137

would understand that. I quickly decided I didn't have much choice, so I carefully moved the phone toward my mouth and meekly replied "Uh ... oh ... kay." At that point the voice was insistent. No matter what I said, I'd need to leave a call-back number. Staying on the line was no longer an option for me. Clearly, I was being punished for my lack of verbal discretion.

I hung up the phone in defeat and debated what to do next. At that point total paranoia set in. How far would the punishment go? Even without leaving a call back number of course they'd know who I was. Maybe I would be denied Medicare benefits. Maybe I would be targeted as an anti-Christian terrorist. God forbid they find out I'm a UU. I slouched back in my chair and uttered the only appropriate words for the whole fiasco, "Jesus fucking Christ!"

This week I overcame my fears and went online to apply. It seemed fairly straight forward. I decided as I was filling in the information it was fitting to shout out a few swears for no reason other than to enjoy the lack of rebuke. I haven't heard yet if my application went through but I'm hopeful and I have learned a lesson: don't swear at automated messaging services; reserve that tor real people.

Jeri Kroll

48: Why Are Your Walking?

I was out for a run/walk several weeks ago and had slowed to a walk near the Walgreens plaza in town when a woman rushed up to me and asked in an accusatory tone, "Why are you walking?" I was immediately taken aback by a stranger rushing up to me and I couldn't figure out exactly why she was questioning me. My mind began to whirl in multiple directions as I tried to come up with an answer for her. Was there something wrong with walking past Walgreens? Was I supposed to be in my car? Was I not supposed to be on my feet pounding away at my joints? Did I even know this woman? She didn't look familiar. The only answer I could come up with was more of a question. "This is what I do?" I finally said.

"Oh, well," she said. "It's just that I saw you way back there running and you looked really good." I was initially relieved when it appeared that all she was trying to do was to give me a compliment. "This is what I do, run ... walk ... run ... walk. I call it ralking". "Well," she declared again in a somewhat accusatory tone. "You looked good." At that point I wasn't sure what to think. On the one hand it was nice that I looked good when I was running, but did I look like a slacker when I was walking? Was it a compliment or a challenge?

True to form, I decided to use her words as a challenge but in a way that might work to my advantage. Last week when I was running in a road race, every

139

time I walked a few paces I heard her voice: "Why are you walking?" "Okay, okay," I responded to the voice in my head, "I'll run. I'll run, and I'll look damn good." In fact, I shaved eight minutes off my time from the previous year!

While I'm sure it would not be a positive direction for me to foster the development of a bunch of voices in my head saying accusatory things, I thought it was worth playing out the idea a bit.

Why are you eating that potato chip? I saw you earlier eating an apple and you looked really good. Why are you watching an old episode of Law and Order? I saw you a couple of nights ago reading a book and you looked really awesome. Why are you drinking martinis? I saw you the other night with one glass of wine and you looked just fine. Maybe that woman could come and stay with me for a few days. We could pin down all my bad habits and come up with healthier alternatives that I could add to my inner dialogue. I could be a new person in no time.

The problem is it wouldn't work. I can't be that perfect. Sometimes I just need junk food and Law and Order and a martini or two and I don't want to have to fight to get it! And when I think about it, I'm not that bad. I might not be able to run all the time, but at least out there, for God's sake.

So now when I'm out ralking, every once in a while, for amusement I ask myself, "Why are you running? I saw you walking back there and you looked just fine."

Jeri Kroll

49: Maybe

Maybe
  1. adverb – possibly but not certainly, perhaps
  2. noun – something that is not known for certain
Merriam Webster

When I was a kid the word "maybe" meant "no."
For example, "Can we get ice cream on the way
home?" "Maybe." There was never any explanation
needed. It wasn't maybe if you're good. Maybe if we
have time. Maybe if the line isn't too long. We were
not stopping for ice cream on the way home.

As an adult I frequently use the word "maybe" but
it's not my way of saying "no", nor in this usage is
it usually a matter of uncertainty as suggested in
its dictionary definition. It's more a matter of trying to envision another person's actions in a
kinder, more gentle way.

For example, if another driver cuts me off in traffic
to take a sudden left turn, I think, "Maybe he's not
from this part of the state. Maybe he's rushing a
loved one to an emergency medical appointment
and he's distraught in addition to possibly being
disoriented geographically."

Or, maybe the woman who did not pick up her
dog's excrement in the park today has been under-
going treatment for a brain tumor and, though

141

normally a responsible pet owner, forgot her poop bags on this one and only occasion.

Of course, I'm most likely dead wrong about both these individuals. He's probably an asshole and she's an inconsiderate shit-head. But isn't it more fun to entertain an alternate reality where people aren't that bad and their sole purpose is not to make your life miserable?

I'll stick with these maybe's. They humor me and leave me feeling good about people.

The other way I often use the word "maybe" is less positive.

For example, maybe the car won't start tomorrow, and I'll miss my long-awaited, very-important, al-most-a-matter-of-life-and-death appointment so I should get up at 3:00 AM just to be sure.

Or, maybe the temperature will drop to 10 below zero during my trip to Florida so I should take my L.L. Bean down jacket, mittens, scarf and wool hat. Boots too – don't forget the boots.

Of course, I'm most likely dead wrong about both these scenarios. The car will start – it's brand-new and I wouldn't die if I had to re-schedule the ap-pointment. It might be chillier in Florida than it normally is but no down and wool are necessary. And no boots – forget the boots.

Maybe I need to get rid of these negative maybes and replace with more positive ones like this:

Maybe the storm which is predicted to drop a foot
of snow on the region will go south ... or maybe
north ... or maybe out to sea.

Or even better maybes may be:
Maybe I'm smarter than I thought.
Maybe I'm going to be amazingly successful.

Whatever way I use the word "maybe," I realize
that intellectually I live in a maybe world, which is
perhaps why I use the word so often. It's not that
there is no certainty anywhere, but there is a lot of
"possibly" and "perhaps".

Truth is not absolute and even if truth is absolute,
our knowledge of it is imperfect.

Maybe I'm wrong, but maybe I'm not.

ABOUT THE AUTHOR

Jeri Kroll is a retired director of professional development in the human service field. She has enjoyed creative writing for as long as she can remember. Her hope is that her short essays and poems will provide encouragement (and laughter) to others on their journey She lives in Ipswich, Massachusetts with her partner, Jodi and dog, Suzie.